Meditating

Jinananda

Meditating

WINDHORSE PUBLICATIONS

Published by Windhorse Publications
11 Park Road, Birmingham, B13 8AB

© Jinananda 2000

Printed by Interprint Ltd
Marsa, Malta
Cover design: Vincent Stokes
Detail of water: Corbis
Detail of sky: Photodisc
Portrait of meditator by Vincent Stokes
Illustrations on p.107: Simon Perry

British Library Cataloguing in Publication Data:
A catalogue record for this book is available from the British Library.
ISBN 1 899579 07 9

CONTENTS

To my son, Antoine, with love

ACKNOWLEDGMENTS

I would like to thank my meditation teachers, Kamalashila and Vajradaka, and my tireless editor, Vidyadevi, who gave my ramblings the lineaments of a book. Thanks also to those who gave encouragement and support and invaluable advice and criticism: Jan Parker, Nagabodhi, Kulananda, Claudia Campos, Kamalashila, and Vessantara, and to Dharmashura, Shantavira, Sara Hagel, and Padmavajri for carrying on the struggle to get a book out of me. And thanks to Nicolas Soames as always. Finally, I must thank all those to whom I have taught meditation over the years, who have stimulated me to keep coming at it afresh.

About the Author

Jinananda, also known as Duncan Steen, was born in 1952 in Bedford, England. Brought up in the Church of England, which he enjoyed (thanks to the music and the Authorised Version), he took up Transcendental Meditation in 1970, and later studied Samkhya yoga in India, before discovering Buddhism in England. He was ordained within the Western Buddhist Order in 1986, when he was given his Buddhist name, which means 'Bliss of the Conqueror'. Since 1990 he has worked as an editor for his teacher, Urgyen Sangharakshita. He is the author of *The Middle Way: The Story of Buddhism* and an English version of Sophocles' *Oedipus the King*, both published by Naxos Audio Books. He has taught meditation and Buddhism at the West London Buddhist Centre for fourteen years.

PREFACE

The importance of the theme 'living a Buddhist life' lies in the fact that the practice of Buddhism is for the whole person. It concerns our actions of body, speech, and mind – no aspect of our life is exempt. The teaching of the Buddha has been summed up in a single phrase, 'actions have consequences'. Our thoughts, words, and deeds all have their effect in the world, for good or ill, creating either happiness or suffering.

Unskilful actions – those proceeding from states of mind based on craving, ill will, and ignorance – create suffering. Skilful actions create happiness and proceed from states of mind based on generosity, love, and wisdom. To be able to recognize and distinguish mental states we need to be aware. So a Buddhist lives, or attempts to live, with awareness, and imbues, or tries to imbue, every area of life with these qualities of generosity, love, and wisdom. It is not an easy task but it is one that gives rise to many benefits.

Buddhist practices – of meditation, ritual, and study of the Dharma (the Buddha's teaching) – are undertaken in order to develop greater awareness and friendliness. In addition, our everyday activities provide infinite opportunities to practise and to change ourselves. In this way we guide and direct the lives we create, both individually and collectively.

I am fortunate to live and work in a retreat centre in a beautiful valley in South Wales. At the head of the valley is a large reservoir, and most days, when on retreat, I walk to the edge and gaze out over the expanse of water. Whatever the day, whatever the weather, there is always some quality of light, of colour, of movement that catches my eye and gives me pleasure. As the retreat progresses and my meditation intensifies, I sometimes experience a deep sense of contentment, a freedom of heart and mind that lets things 'be' in their beauty and yet derives such delight and richness from them.

At the same time I find myself becoming increasingly appreciative of those around me. While I may never have met some of the retreatants before, and may indeed have felt some resistance to being with a new group of people, I begin to have a stronger sense of our common humanity, to take a greater interest in the experiences of others and the concerns they bring with them, and to empathize with the efforts they are making to change what may be the habits of a lifetime. At times I find my heart flooding with affection and warmth towards everyone practising alongside me.

This delight in the world and in other people is, I know, directly related to meditation practice. Meditation is not the only form of Buddhist practice through which we can develop greater awareness and positive states of mind, but it is probably the most immediate and accessible way of developing those qualities. Anybody who has sufficient interest and is capable of sitting still for more than a few minutes at a time can begin to practise meditation and experience its benefits.

Meditation puts us in touch with ourselves, and at times this means getting in touch with the pains as well as the pleasures of our experience. Our dissatisfactions are often covered over by all sorts of distractions, and meditation reveals the experience underlying those distractions. Experiencing that dissatisfaction is painful, but meditation, as well as uncovering it, gives us a way to a more truly satisfying experience. That is the starting point of this book. After describing how to prepare for meditation, Jinananda describes two basic meditation practices that offer tools for the transformation of mind and heart, as well as giving us practical tips on how to take one's meditation further.

Having been involved with an urban Buddhist centre for many years, and now living at a country retreat centre, I have seen so many people change and become happier through the influence of meditation and other Buddhist practices, I have seen superficial and restricting personalities drop away, deep-seated attitudes to life overturned, and clearer, more authentic individuals emerge, able to relate more fully to themselves and to others.

This alone would be sufficient reason to meditate. But when we realize that the sustained and consistent practice of meditation can also lead to transcendental insight, a profound and irreversible change in our being that enables us to see through the causes of suffering, it becomes clear that meditation is a practice of inestimable value.

Maitreyi
Tiratanaloka
Wales
March 2000

1

INTRODUCTION

Wonders are many, but none more
Wondrous and unfathomed than Man,
The wanderer, who strides the rage
Of winter winds over grey seas.
  Sophocles, *Antigone*

A curious assumption lies behind our pursuit of happiness. We assume that in order to find life deeply satisfying we have to find things – movies, relationships, food, drink, holidays, sex, books, meditation – that will deliver this deep satisfaction. The conclusion we draw from this is that the more gratifying experiences we can fit into as short a time as possible, the happier we shall be. Indeed, we are prepared to go to a lot of trouble – even a lot of misery – to get our hands on as many of life's satisfying goods as we can.

But if we look a little more closely at our pleasures, they consist in those activities – whether we call them work or play – to which we offer no resistance. Someone who is fully absorbed in watching a film, changing a nappy, or climbing a mountain is happy because she experiences no conflict. She doesn't feel boredom, resentment, shame, anxiety, greed.... Her mind isn't somewhere else.

Meditation is the practical application of this simple idea: that satisfaction, happiness, absorption, is not the end-product of some gratifying thing or experience, but a way of going about things. Happiness is something we bring to life, not something life delivers to us. This may sound like a nice idea, but it is a profoundly strange one. It suggests that we can develop the state of absorption we call happiness independently of whether or not we find ourselves in happy circumstances. And this is where meditation comes in. We can discover happiness as a resource for the service of the life around us rather than devoting our life to the vain pursuit of some kind of problem-free happiness .

The purpose of meditation is to take full possession of our experience of the heart's unutterable intervention in the world. It helps us to inhabit the real world instead of semi-consciously inhabiting our own world inside the 'outside' world and muddling up the two. It is only in the full presence of the inner world that the outer world can be fully present to us.

The experience of feeling disconnected from things, from other people, from a deeper appreciation of the world around us, is really the experience of a discon-nected self. The faster our minds flick from one channel of our experience to another, looking for something sufficiently gripping to hold our attention, the more fragmentary and superficial that experience tends to be.

This vampiric searching for nourishment from the life around us is essentially unconscious. In *Dracula*, the sinister count is recognized as a vampire by the fact that he has no reflection in a mirror; his nature is that he never sees himself. He is also immortal – he has refused the gift of impermanence – but his fear of loss, of disconnection, actually disconnects him from life and light. And only two things will reduce him to a handful of dust: exposing him to daylight or driving a stake through his heart. To put it less drastically, the life drained of meaning that he symbolizes is vulnerable to the light of awareness, and the opening of the heart. And the two basic practices of Buddhist meditation I shall be introducing in this book are concerned with cultivating these qualities of awareness and open-heartedness.

Both are straightforward exercises for ordinary life. However, I have raised the image of Count Dracula in his life or death struggle with his old adversary, Dr Van Helsing, in order to emphasize that meditation represents something quite uncompromising, a radical change of direction for the psyche. At the same time, this profound change of direction involves a patient acceptance, an openness, a great tenderness towards our own states of mind as they start to reveal themselves to us in meditation. In traditional Buddhist terms, wisdom comes with an equally uncompromising compassion, which excludes no one, not even ourselves.

There is no one experiencing our mental states from outside them. We *are* them. If we want to experience different states, we have to become them. And that process begins the moment we form an intention to meditate. Meditation is a practice, not a performance. You can start whenever you can clear a short space in your day. Now, for example. To try it out, all you have to do is put aside for a few moments all the things you have to worry about today and sit down: still, relaxed, softly awake, eyes gently closed. Then begin to appreciate these empty moments in themselves. These moments are owed to no one. Nor are they an investment for some future pay-off. You don't even have to make the most of them. Savour them at your ease. Just watch them bubble out of your mind ... then notice the baggage of reactions with which you want to weigh them down.... Now see if you can be patient enough to release the bright, steady, spacious quality that is present in those moments.

PART ONE

PREPARING FOR MEDITATION

1

STEPPING OUT OF THE WORLD

In every consulting room, there ought to be two rather
frightened people: the patient and the psychoanalyst. If
they are not, one wonders why they are bothering to
find out what everyone knows.
W.R. Bion

Why meditate? To let go of stress? To become more
focused? To fathom the mysteries of the universe? Whatever your purpose may be – and it will probably change
over time – you won't be able to meditate without it.
Meditation does not appear to be a very useful activity
viewed from one's 'got a busy day' perspective, and the
effect of meditating, however powerful, can seem to fade
all too quickly. It is such an utterly different activity that
our ordinary way of being does not recognize it, so we
are going to have to find ways to shape our intention into
a purpose that our everyday mind can readily appreciate. Whatever name we give our purpose – calming

down, for example, or becoming more focused, even exploring the mysteries of human consciousness – it is a good idea to keep it in mind. The easiest way to do this is to attend a regular meditation group. The quotation at the beginning of the book is intended to be a bit of a warning that finding peace of mind can be a long and occasionally difficult haul, and it is only fair to say that most people who try to meditate without regular contact with others on the same journey will drift back to port.

What may start off as a bit of a struggle to fit meditation into your everyday life can become an understanding, even a rapport, between the two areas of experience. You can be sure that your meditation is beginning to take off when you become aware that it is having an effect on the rest of your life. But you will also gradually become aware that your everyday life – particularly the way you treat other people as well as the way you treat yourself – is having an effect on your meditation. It should begin to become clear, then, that ethics is no less a training of the mind than is meditation. That is to say, our actions are not just things we do; at the same time as they express our being they also change it.

The fundamental Buddhist insight is that nothing happens in isolation. So there is a connection between meditation and whatever else you do. But even though the aim is to stay centred, aware, and kind in the storms and doldrums of everyday activity, anyone who meditates will need to find a way to navigate the transition from ordinary life to meditation. It helps to establish a non-negotiable time to meditate. That will help you, and everyone else who is part of your life, to support your intention. If you have been rushing around, you will need to step down a few gears before you meditate, perhaps by engaging in some quiet, simple, unhurried activity: sweeping the floor, say, or watering the garden, or having a cup of tea, or doing a few yoga stretches.

Now you are ready to start. So – where would be a good place? If you are going to close your eyes it won't matter where you sit – right? Well, let's think about it.

When you sit down to meditate for the first time, it is natural to feel a little apprehensive. This is a good thing. It means you are open to the possibility that something new is going to happen. If you feel 'at home' with meditation, if you have settled down with something safe and familiar, you are not going to be so open to this possibility. To maintain something of the wide-eyed freshness that the Zen tradition calls 'beginner's mind', we need to nourish this slight sense of apprehensiveness.

Our knowledge has banished our fear of the old gods, but in meditation we need to reconnect with a sense of moving through a world we don't understand. We are entering a different realm in which different rules apply; we are in some sense stepping out of the world in which we usually live. At least, we should feel as if this is what we are doing. So we need to fix a regular exit point in the onward rush of our day. We need to make a time in our day when everything stops (or, perhaps, first thing in the morning, before everything starts), and a quiet, still space in our home, free from external distraction.

And yet, as we shall see, the main distraction is always oneself, the chatter of the mind reassuring itself in the dark. The quiet place we are seeking is an inner stillness, yet to be discovered. It is in support of our search for this place within that we need to create an external space that is uncharted and at the same time protected. How do we do this? The answer is rather traditional. We make it a sacred place, a ritual space.

Meditating with others helps to generate a more powerful ritual space, but you can create your own by setting aside a corner of your home for meditation, and placing there something to suggest the state of mind you are trying to nurture – a picture, a vase of flowers, or whatever. Buddhists meditate in front of a shrine, simple or elaborate. This provides a kind of gateway to the mind, as well as arousing the sense of awe and reverence that comes naturally to all possessors of human consciousness, but which gets lost in the dust of our passing days. The central place on most shrines is devoted to some sort of Buddha image, an image that conveys the point of what one is doing more clearly and immediately than any number of words.

Whether you call yourself a Buddhist or not, sitting in front of a Buddha image (called a *rupa*, which means 'form') does not signify that you have turned your life over to some clunking religiosity. You can meditate effectively – indeed, you can practise Buddhism generally – without a firm belief in anything apart from whatever will keep you practising. Buddhism is a practice. There is no need to embrace a lot of strange ideas. Far from being exotic, it points the way home, giving us the space to appreciate those things that are so humdrum we usually don't even see them. It means opening up the gaps between what we usually think of as the main events of the day, finding value in the moments between our practical affairs, jumping the tram-lines of our own narrow concerns and discovering that there really is – if we attend to it – a whole world, so to speak, out there.

A Buddha image on a shrine is not an idol. It does not represent some sort of god. It represents the open-endedness of the exploration of the mind and heart, a recognition that there is no limit to that process and that we cannot therefore conceive of where it is leading – or indeed what deeper processes may be going on under-neath whatever sense we are making of it.

This perspective is surprisingly practical. If you find yourself losing heart when you don't seem to be getting the results you envisaged, or if you start to get over-excited and lose concentration when you seem to be doing well – and this is bound to happen sometimes – it is important to have a way of shifting your focus beyond short-term goals.

One way to do this is to dedicate the meditation to its unknowable dimension: to offer it to the Buddha, who represents the ideal of what you are trying to do with your life. You are then free to get on with the meditation. You aren't trapped with some rather cramped and su-perficial mental states, nor are you floating off on in-flated fantasies of being on the verge of Enlightenment.

Whether it seems to be going well or not, you can relax and just keep putting one foot in front of the other.

It is to encourage this open-ended perspective that Buddhists usually bow to the shrine before meditating, and perhaps offer flowers or incense. Bowing, like chanting verses or mantras, is a simple way of putting yourself, heart and soul, into the meditation practice. And we need to have feeling, even passion, for what we are doing. If our intention to meditate is just an idea, it won't keep us going long; it will be like the kind of New Year's resolution that is forgotten by the middle of January.

Whether you think in terms of connecting with your positive motivation within, or have a sense of invoking the help of a living presence beyond or outside you – and either of these can be expressed through bowing to a shrine – it basically comes to the same thing. You are calling forth something to take care of your practice which is outside the control of the conceptualizing mind.

You can connect with your inspiration and purpose in other ways, too; by reading a few lines of poetry, say, or bringing to mind someone whose qualities you admire. This needn't be some big-deal Buddhist. You can look at a child banging the floor with a wooden spoon, or scribbling with an orange crayon. Then look for your own innocent pleasure, your own simplicity and absorption. The secret of meditation lies in the preparation. Have a sense that you are dedicating yourself – dedicating this time and this place – to meditation.

2

COMING TO OUR SENSES

Love's mysteries in souls do grow,
But yet the body is his book.
John Donne, 'The Ecstasy'

It may appear that your body is doing nothing much in meditation: you leave it sitting on the ground while your mind gets on with it. However, this is not the way Buddhism works. The Buddhist agenda is not to free up one's true spiritual nature from the trammels of material form. According to Buddhism, mind and body arise in dependence upon each other. They are different categories, not separate realities. Most of the time we treat our bodies just as the apparatus by means of which we experience the world as feeling, react to it as emotion, and work our will upon it as action. It's a sort of go-between, a resource to be used. But in meditation you don't try to concentrate the mind on its own. Concentration also involves bringing your physical experience together. The body is attended to from within – that is, we begin to occupy it fully, we begin to enjoy being at home in it.

Strange to say, this is not where we usually are. Our normal experience of life is a sort of out-of-the-body experience. We are elsewhere. We have a wonderful capacity to check out of our present situation and try out others in our imagination, and sometimes we use that as a sort of escape mechanism. If we are not altogether present, this is generally because we don't want to be. We don't want to feel all our feelings, or express all our emotions.

We don't really escape them, however. They are registered unconsciously in the body, and manifest as tension in certain areas – the jaw, perhaps, or the hands, the hips or the stomach. This tension blocks the flow of energy to other areas and results in various forms of stiffness or slackness of gait and posture. The English language recognizes this close connection between states of mind and states of body with expressions like 'heartless', 'stiff-necked', and 'cold feet'. Our body shape changes from day to day depending on our mood and general state of mind, and as we grow older it bears clearer traces of our personality and our approach to life. In this way our mental states become embodied.

All this is simply to say that the mind and the body constitute the two ends of a single process, and that we can start to change ourselves through the body as well as through the mind. The focusing of ourselves that the Buddhist tradition calls mindfulness involves a focus of posture as well as of mind; it is also 'bodyfulness' (and heartfulness). So the first task in meditation is to release tension, to relax, and to open up the body. That will help the thoughts and feelings associated with those tensions to emerge gradually into consciousness.

You may like to do a little physical exercise before you meditate – a few yoga stretches or *ch'i-kung* exercises, say – to begin the process of entering into your physical experience. Then find a good meditation posture – one that embodies the state of mind you intend to cultivate. It will be secure and stable, but also comfortable and responsive, relaxed and energetic. Think of someone carrying a pitcher of water on her head. The energy of the body is unified, focused, bringing a natural dignity and strength to the posture. No part of the spine is rigid or slumped.

Sitting cross-legged or kneeling is generally best, supported by cushions or a stool. Adjust the height of the cushions to make sure you can feel the support of the ground through your knees and legs, while at the same time the whole length of your spine is free and flexible. You may have to sit with a little physical discomfort to begin with, just as you may have to sit with uncomfortable mental states, but in the long run this sort of posture should prove the easiest to maintain for long periods. Your hands should be supported in some way – perhaps on a blanket folded around you. If you like, you can place one hand in the other, but don't interlock your fingers, as that can lead to the development of tension in the hands. Tilt your chin slightly downwards, to maintain the flow of energy through your neck, while allowing your back and neck to stay relaxed (see p.107).

If you need to sit in a chair, it is best not to lean against the back. Putting a thin piece of wood or a couple of books under the back feet of the chair to tilt it forward a little will take pressure off the base of your spine. Plant both feet firmly on the floor. If you are ill or in pain and need to sit or lie in bed, you can still meditate. Most people, whatever their meditation posture, occasionally experience physical pain in meditation. This can often be relieved just by a little movement. If you have chronic pain, try to find a middle way between pushing the pain out of your awareness and letting it dominate. Try to allow it its place among other aspects of your experience. This is easier said than done, but there are no easy answers in meditation. Meditation is designed to take us beyond the sense-based experience in which pleasure and pain can dominate the mind; but of course pain can seem to hold us in the realm of the senses rather more insistently than physical pleasure. All one can offer is the traditional Buddhist view, which is that pain provides a much stronger motivation to make one's meditation effective.

When you have found as comfortable a position as you can, you are ready to begin meditating. Close your eyes, or settle your gaze softly on the floor in front of you (either is fine). Sitting still at once reduces sensory input – as does closing the eyes, of course – and you are left with an increased awareness of the thoughts and feelings that usually get tangled up in all that input. The way to begin working with those thoughts and feelings is in fact through exploring one's physical experience. In this way you begin to touch base with the present moment.

Surprisingly, perhaps, it can take quite a bit of practice to become really aware of your body. To begin with, you can find yourself sitting atop your physical experience as if it were alien territory. This territory cannot be forcibly reoccupied; you need to approach it not like a business takeover or a military coup but as you would approach something that requires a great deal of sensitivity – birdwatching, perhaps. Your body is not an object but your own immediate experience. Looking around your inner world of sense experience, wait for steady, clear sensations to make themselves felt just as they are, as sensations.

Most of our raw energy comes from the lower parts of our body, and meditation needs energy. Your posture should therefore carry a sense of belonging to the earth. On this solid base, your torso can rise up with a sense of lightness, buoyancy, spaciousness, a sense that you can take up as much space as you need, that you can fill it with your presence, that there is always room to expand your boundaries. Gradually you experience your body as a single, integrated whole.

Take time over this. Just sitting still helps to create a calmer mental state. Like a still lake, the quiet body offers a mirror to the mind. There is no need to run after your experience, or work anything out, or imagine anything. Just give attention to every corner of your sensory world, from the toes to the scalp, letting go of any tension or dullness, awakening and relaxing your whole body. Bring awareness to your skin, muscles, organs, even your bones. As you do so, your mind will also begin to relax and come alive.

To get an impression of the kind of posture you are aiming for, look at an infant sitting up. The back is straight and at the same time soft. The whole body is relaxed yet totally focused on the object of the child's fascinated attention. A child is as deeply rooted as a tree, and reaches up to the world as easily and naturally as a tree's branches reach up to the sun. Above all, the posture is not fixed, but totally alive.

PART TWO

AWARENESS

3

WHAT IS MINDFULNESS?

The secret motive of the absent-minded is to be innocent while guilty.
Saul Bellow, *More Die of Heartbreak*

Once you are relatively present, collected, centred, still, and aware, you are ready to begin a specific technique.

Meditation practices are designed to develop qualities of mind that, to some extent, we already possess. They do this through deliberately connecting what we are doing at any moment with what we are doing the next. This makes us aware of the conflicts that make our experience so disconnected, and this awareness of itself has the power to resolve those conflicts.

The first aim of any meditation technique is to develop a continuous flow of positive mental states. The key word here is 'continuous'. Everyone has positive mental states from time to time – we all know what it is to be happy, content, joyful, kind, and generous. Meditation involves consciously sustaining a continuous flow of such positive states. So the starting point of meditation is to become aware of the flow of what is going on in the mind – whether positive or negative – so that we can learn to direct that flow.

If we think of meditation as an experience we want to *have*, we won't get far. We will just be persisting in our habitual strategy in life, which is to focus on experiences that press our reward buttons, and to ignore or flinch from those that don't. Meditation does not just deliver another experience. It runs a thread of awareness through them. We may have all sorts of wonderful – or occasionally unsettling – experiences while we are meditating, but meditation itself is the activity of connecting up our experience into what we call awareness.

We develop this attentiveness by focusing on a particular object or series of objects, either external – a candle flame, say, or an image or sound – or some kind of internal physical or psycho-physical process, whether the breath or the emotions or some more esoteric internal object. Whatever the object, the act of focusing will gradually channel the attention in a single direction.

The name given to the quality of focus we are aiming for is mindfulness. This is not a forced concentration, but a gathering of attention around the object of meditation. Mindfulness is the drawing together of all one's faculties. It is not just awareness, but an intentional awareness, a directed attentiveness. It involves being aware of what has happened, being watchful for what may be about to happen, and being true to one's purpose. As we become more and more aware, more and more of our energy is channelled into the present moment. Being present is a matter not so much of concentrating on the moment as of concentrating the energies you bring to it. The result is a deeply fulfilling experience of even the simplest activities. The Zen tradition approaches the goal of Buddhism very much in this way:

How wonderful, how miraculous.
I chop wood, I carry water.

This kind of quiet miracle is perhaps most accessible to us in the peace and spaciousness of nature. But we could just as well cry out 'How wonderful, how miraculous. I catch the bus home, I make the kid's tea.' Mindfulness brings a depth of colour, resonance, and meaning to life, wherever you are, whatever you are doing, and whatever is happening, whether banal or dramatic.

The idea is not to start trying to squeeze quiet miracles out of everyday activities but simply to attend to your experience. You become aware not just of objects, but of objects being attended to. You become aware that what you are looking at or hearing or smelling or tasting or feeling or thinking *is being* looked at or heard or tasted or felt or thought about. It's that simple. In fact, you can start now; not later, when you've bought a meditation cushion or when the children have grown up. Now. Be aware that you are reading this. It is incredibly easy. The difficult bit is to carry on doing it. The practice is to keep returning to it. Little by little, we will learn to join up the dots of our momentary flashes of awareness.

4

THE MINDFULNESS OF BREATHING

Like a long-legged fly upon the stream
His mind moves upon silence.
W.B. Yeats, 'Long-Legged Fly'

The most widely practised mindfulness meditation in the Buddhist tradition is the Mindfulness of Breathing. There are various reasons for the importance of this practice. Breathing is deeply and subtly enjoyable. It is the most fundamental experience of being alive. It is where we connect with the outside world most immediately. Each breath we take is a reminder that our life is on loan. Every few moments we are given a refreshing new lungful of air to enjoy. At the same time we are always letting go of the breath, and one day we will let go of it for the last time.

The breath also reveals how the mind connects with the body – as when, say, we hold the breath, or release it slowly while performing some delicate task. The breath is where we connect with our feelings and emotions most directly – when our breathing quickens, when we gasp or even stop breathing momentarily, when we laugh or whistle or sing.

We often 'take a deep breath' to collect ourselves before doing something challenging, and this is quite a good way to start the Mindfulness of Breathing. Once you have settled yourself down to meditate and brought your awareness to your physical experience, just take a few deep breaths to bring your breathing into the general frame of your attention.

After that, just allow your breathing to be natural. The meditation involves attending to the breath, not trying to control it or do anything with it. Your body will reach for each breath by itself. Just let it come and go in its own time, whilst keeping it steadily in mind.

To help us achieve this steady focus, the practice is usually divided into several stages. The following version has four. Allow about five minutes for each stage when you're learning the meditation.

THE FIRST STAGE

In the first stage of the practice, you number each out-breath. After an out-breath, count 'one' (mentally, not out loud). After the next breath count 'two', and so on, until you have counted ten breaths. Then go back to 'one' and count ten breaths again, and so on. If you lose count, or realize that you have counted beyond ten, just start again at 'one'.

The counting is useful because it gives you early warning of the mind wandering – you will be aware of losing count before you are aware of having drifted off – as well as an instant yardstick for your initial attention span. In themselves, the numbers are not an important part of the practice; they just pin your attention to the breath until you can maintain some continuity of awareness without them. So keep the counting quite muted (or if you are more of a visualizer, introduce the numbers unobtrusively in the corner of the 'canvas'). The breath is the star of the show – indeed, you can attend to the breath as if you were listening to music. Don't try to control your breathing – just let it go its own way and follow it.

Nor is there any need to worry about the mind wandering. It *will* wander. You could imagine that you have tethered your mind like a goat in the middle of a field. You allow it plenty of rope so that it can wander about, but all the time you are gently drawing it in. The challenge is to bring your attention back to the breathing as soon as you realize it has wandered away. That is what mindfulness is. At the same time, see if you can feel the breath creating a sense of space and light in which any tangles of tension, impatience, or dullness may loosen and dissolve.

THE SECOND STAGE

In the second stage count before each in-breath: 'one' (breathe in, breathe out), 'two' (breathe in, breathe out), and so on, up to 'ten', then start again at 'one'. That is to say, anticipate what is going to happen instead of marking what has already happened. This change is subtle, but it reflects quite an important shift. In fact, subtle though it is, it tells us something crucial about the nature of awareness. One could even say that truly ethical behaviour has its basis in this kind of shift – the shift from being aware that something has happened to being aware that it is about to happen. Awareness after the event – after you have reacted to something – is a start: it's the beginning of mindfulness. But the aim is to catch the impulse in the mind *before* it is translated into speech or action. Then, finally, you are in the driving seat: your actions are your own and you are taking responsibility for them.

But you still don't go chasing after the breath. It's more like you are looking out for it as it gradually emerges at the centre of your attention, whilst around it is a general awareness of the whole body. From time to time it may be obscured by distractions, but these are like clouds passing across the sky of the mind. The breath is always there behind them, like the sun behind the clouds, and your body is relaxed and alive, and immovable as a mountain. Clouds will always tend to form around mountains, and storms will beat about you in that rarefied atmosphere. But don't let the clouds – the distractions – discourage you. Implicit in the *awareness* of being in a negative mental state is the seed of its opposite. Look for the stillness at the heart of your awareness of being restless.

THE THIRD STAGE
Now fade out the counting altogether. You may find that you are sufficiently present – your energies sufficiently integrated – for just sitting with the breath to be very satisfying in itself, and that is the aim of this stage. You

just feel the breath coming and going like the waves of the sea. You don't watch it, you are aware of it – your awareness is with it, within it. Welcome each moment in with the breath, and see it out again. Feel your belly drawing energy up with the breath. Allow your chest and shoulders to open as the tide of the breath turns.

This stage is like watching a child on a swing: there is a feeling of pleasure tempered with care and watchfulness. Try to get a sense of the breath as a whole, as it moves through the cycle of inhalation and exhalation. Feel the movement of the whole torso. Pay particular attention to the turn of the breath – this is where you are most likely to lose concentration. Experiment with allowing your attention to deepen and broaden. If you drift off, draw your attention back to the breath. Focus *in* the breath, rather than *on* it.

THE FOURTH STAGE

In the final stage of the meditation, focus on a small detail of the breathing process: the point where you experience the breath entering or leaving your body, usually a subtle flow of sensation around the nostrils. This is quite tricky: the mind has to ride the constantly changing flow of sensation with a very delicate touch. You can't grab at it or hold on to it; when you try, it's already gone. It is always going and all you can do is let it go. But you can't afford to allow your attention to waver for a moment. You have to be absolutely relaxed, and at the same time completely attentive. You release the mind, and at the same time engage it more closely. The breath is now hardly felt as an object at all. You cannot separate yourself from it; you are within it, absorbed in it.

ENDING THE MEDITATION

At the end of the meditation you naturally have to disengage from the breath and allow other things to come to your attention. Take your time with this transition; plan your time so that you don't have to leap up and rush away to do something else. And try to stay with a sense of being concentrated, fully present, attentive, alert to your purpose. If you meditate in the morning, try to wear the fragrance of your meditation throughout the day. This is as important as the meditation practice itself, and why meditators usually try to slow down and simplify their lives: to find the space to be aware.

The Mindfulness of Breathing seems a simple enough exercise, and may sound rather a dull one. But it is not really an activity of such paint-drying monotony. If we attend to it carefully and closely, we find that the breath is never the same experience; it is always new, always changing. And it turns out not to be like mental press-ups because it is not really about watching the breath. It is about watching the mind, watching oneself. Meditation gradually makes it vividly apparent that our experience is not some kind of objective process. We create it. When we think we are experiencing something, what we are really experiencing is – in a sense – ourselves. So the breath is not really an 'object' at all. The breath is also the mind.

5

EVERYDAY MINDFULNESS

O why do you walk through the fields in gloves,
Missing so much and so much?
Frances Cornford, 'To a Fat Lady seen from the Train'

If you want to find the meaning, stop chasing after so
many things.
Ryokan, *One Robe, One Bowl*

The Buddhist tradition of walking meditation has its origin in the Buddha's teaching that one should always try to be aware what one is doing – standing, sitting, walking, or lying down. This most basic level of mindfulness may sound like something we naturally do already, but in practice we all have the experience of somehow having moved from A to B without having noticed we have done so. One minute you're sitting in front of the television, the next you're in the kitchen putting the kettle on, and you have no idea how you got there. It is as if something beyond our control is making our decisions for us.

Walking meditation is one traditional way of starting to bring more awareness to bodily activity. You walk quite slowly, limiting visual input by focusing on the ground in front of you. As traditionally practised, the walking has no destination, no purpose beyond itself. A Zen teacher has described it as being like carefully sewing a robe, each footstep a finely-judged stitch. This beautiful image emphasizes an important aesthetic dimension to this practice. It connects our mindfulness practice to the world of our everyday activities, and in doing so gathers our ragged experience of the world into a beautiful sustained presence.

Mindfulness is a practice for every day, all the time. We can bring awareness to all our activities. And when we have a little space, we can allow ourselves to *be* spacious – not just fill the space with vague, half-conscious distractions. Mindfulness is about remembering, coming back to ourselves, returning to our purpose, and setting up the conditions in which awareness will deepen. We are gradually moving from an awareness that is triggered more or less accidentally to one that is self-generating.

One way to start this process is to keep a diary: you then naturally start to notice more. You can also decide that every time you walk through a doorway, or go up or down stairs, or hear the church bells, you will use that experience to remind yourself to be aware. When you hear the telephone ringing, you can remember your connection with other people and resolve to pay attention to the quality of your communication before you pick up the receiver. You have to be determined to keep trying to make these connections – it's all too easy to forget for days at a time – but, with practice, anything that happens regularly in your life can be turned into a wake-up call.

A traditional Buddhist exercise is to verbalize your awareness, to say to yourself, 'Holding the warm cup … sipping the tea … thinking about lunch … putting the cup down … turning to the book again … here, now, this.' The verbalization is just a tool, of course, and the less intrusive it is, the more awareness you can bring to what you are doing. But it's important not to get too precious about everyday mindfulness if one is to avoid turning it into an exercise in alienation. It shouldn't become a cold mental clamp on our experience.

Mindfulness involves protecting yourself from distractions; but bear in mind that it can be quite contagious. Do not underestimate the power of mindfulness on others, or the effect that others who practise mindfulness can have on you. The best support for your practice, as Buddhists down the ages have always recognized, is regular contact with those who also practise mindfulness.

In some ways mindfulness outside meditation is very different from – although related to – mindfulness within it. Instead of the mind responding to its own processes, the self is responding to the world, particularly in terms of ethics. As you become more conscious that your experience always contains two poles – subject and object, self and other – you start to appreciate that it always consists of relationship. Our experience is not just to be consumed; it is to be listened to – for at every moment something is being asked of us. Mindfulness involves an appreciation of whatever we do and who-ever we meet – however difficult or straightforward we may find that situation – as giving us something to work with. It means attending to small details, respecting the simple commodities of existence – a chair, toast and butter, tea, appetite. It connects the world we know, neatly packaged like this book, with the world we don't know, the one that is happening. Meditation is a vital training for the mind, but what it is working with in the end is the relationship between the self and the world. The transformation of the mind is the transformation of that relationship.

PART THREE

KINDNESS

6

METTA

While on the shop and street I gazed
My body of a sudden blazed;
And twenty minutes more or less
It seemed, so great my happiness,
That I was blessed and could bless.
  W.B. Yeats, 'Vacillation' IV

THE CULTIVATION OF EMOTIONS

The *Metta Bhavana*, the development of universal loving-kindness, is as fundamental a meditation practice as the Mindfulness of Breathing. Here, though, the object of attention is the flow, not of the breath, but of the emotions. And we don't just attend to the emotions; we actively cultivate certain emotions in particular.

So how do we feel about cultivating emotions? The very idea seems artificial. We want to be authentic, and we tend to distrust people who are too emotionally dextrous. But suppressing or strangling our emotions is not going to help us to be authentic. The middle way here is to attend to emotions more carefully: to be aware of the feelings we experience, and give direction to the emotional response we find emerging out of that experience.

We often use the words 'feeling' and 'emotion' as though they mean the same thing, but, when it comes to meditation, it is important to distinguish between them. We cannot choose our feelings: we have no choice whether something that happens to us produces a pleasant or an unpleasant feeling. But emotion is different. It is an action – the action of making something of one's feelings. For example, to walk out of a warm house into the bitter wind of a winter's day may feel unpleasant, and you can't do anything about that. But reactions like tensing yourself up against the cold and grumbling that you hate winter, or snapping out of it and trying to be positive, clearly involve some element of choice. Indeed, if you can be a little more sensitive and aware, you can perhaps come up with more interesting emotional options than either of these.

If we can bring our awareness closer to where our emotional choices are being made, in the secrecy of the heart, we can make those choices more creatively. The Metta Bhavana involves caring about the way one responds to the world. It is the cultivation not of feelings but of emotions, not of experiences but of actions – because our choices of action are initially made at an emotional level. So one has to stop confusing feeling with emotion, or at least recognize that there are two processes going on in any emotional 'experience', which is why it is so useful to slow it all down through meditation, and try to take it frame by frame.

Because we don't tend to experience emotion separately from feeling, we rarely identify emotions as matters of choice: they blur into the area of feelings, where we have no choice. This leaves us unable to choose our emotional responses. At the very moment we feel something painful, for example, all too often we try to evade that experience by producing an emotional reaction to it, like anger, fear, or guilt. This in turn may be too uncomfortable to experience, so we override it with some other, more acceptable response: 'I'm not angry, I'm just surprised.' Whole areas of emotion can be overrun, and we never know they've gone. Through such unconscious flinching from our experience, we can completely lose touch with the present moment.

What we think of as real emotion is often crude and superficial, expressing blockbuster feelings. This is perhaps particularly the case with men. Often we are not sure what we feel until we are overtaken by some quite strong emotional reaction; and even when we are aware of an emotional response, we are not always sure what it is. Sometimes we are too identified with our emotions to be aware of them; sometimes we deny them altogether.

There are some advantages in being able to override emotions – it can help us to get things done – but to assume on the basis of this practical ability that emotions can always be a secondary consideration is a mistake. Whether we are conscious of them or not, it is our emotions that make our decisions for us. They determine the quality of our life, the nature of our relationship to the world, and the direction in which our energy moves. All our experience is felt; everything we do comes, whether we know it or not, from the heart. Reason is a vital tool, but if we are not aware of the emotions informing and directing it, we are probably misusing it.

THE DEVELOPMENT OF UNIVERSAL LOVING-KINDNESS

Getting in touch with emotions, rather than guessing or assuming or trying to avoid them, and reclaiming a measure of freedom within them, is the engine-room of the Metta Bhavana. However, for the direction and momentum of this practice we need to look at its ultimate goal.

Bhavana means 'cultivation of' and *metta* means 'love'. This is not love as we usually understand the term. I may love my wife, my children, my friends, and my country; I may love truffle chocolates, Arsenal, Jacques Tati, and Scarlatti; but I hardly need to cultivate this kind of love, however important and estimable (or not) the objects of my partiality may be.

Metta is different. It is impartial love – love for all living beings – and as such it is something we may not experience very often. It is emotion, but not as we know it. Metta does not somehow obliterate our likes and dislikes, but as we become practised at developing it, our likes and dislikes will become steadily less absolute, less rigid, less brittle. The peaks and troughs of our emotions are still there, but we become aware that they are only the surface of the ocean of our deeper connection with all that lives.

The aim of the Metta Bhavana, according to the Buddha in the *Metta Sutta*, is to develop towards all living beings the response that a mother has towards her only child. So this image suggests three things. Firstly, it is not a matter of developing a sort of lordly benevolence; it is about fashioning a living, hands-on, unbreakable bond with all other beings. In a sense it goes beyond an emotional response – it is simply the reality of the situation. Secondly, we make metta real not by imagining what it is like but by bringing awareness to real emotions. And, thirdly, metta moves naturally towards action. The fact that a mother's activities are centred around the needs of her child gives her a very down-to-earth, businesslike attitude.

The experience of metta is a natural, if rarely visited, extension of our most characteristically human qualities. Most of us are concerned for the welfare of people with whom we have no apparent connection. We are troubled by the sufferings of victims of oppression throughout the world, and moved when they rise up to claim their freedom. We express solidarity with others by giving to charity, donating blood, voluntary work, and so on.

So we have metta to hand; but we may find it hard to let it in very far. Metta loosens up our identity, and we don't want this to happen. We want to hang on to our likes and dislikes, we even want them to be absolute, incontrovertible. But the fact is that if my circumstances were ever so slightly different, I should have a completely different set of friends and views and attachments. I might be a Christian, or a Hindu, or a Muslim.

I could so easily find myself on the other side of the fence. Indeed, a full experience of metta leads to the realization that there isn't really a fence there at all.

Metta is a faculty of the heart, an emotional attitude, a way of responding to living beings wherever and whenever they come to our attention. It is not speculative or abstract. But nor is it gloopy or sentimental. What others need from us is not emotionalism, but awareness and consideration. Metta is about being able to break out of our own subjectivity and engage with another person's needs – i.e. as a practical consideration rather than just as a feeling. And this going out from ourselves produces, paradoxically, a sense of deeper integration within us. Conversely, when we cut off from others, we cut off from ourselves. This is not just theory. If you are impatient with someone, for example, you can feel this happening: something shuts down in your mind. You don't want to know.

Practising the Metta Bhavana gives us a more precise awareness of other people's feelings. You find that you are able to deal more effectively with people you dislike or with whom you are upset. You aren't taken over by free-floating emotions that are not embedded in a deeper context of awareness and care, and you are better able to deal with other people's difficult emotions as well. Above all, you enjoy people more. The child in us will always enjoy being loved, but for an adult, finding love is finding a capacity to love, to appreciate, even to relish, other people.

7

KNOWING HOW WE FEEL

*I became very interested in those thoughts of mine that
I could never catch … they were a dim sort of feeling.*
Ted Hughes, *Poetry in the Making*

You begin the Metta Bhavana as you begin any meditation, by bringing to mind your overall purpose and then
tuning into an awareness of your body. Next, you begin
to develop another kind of sensitivity, one that is closely
related to becoming aware of the body. You begin to get
a sense of what emotions are stirring.

Emotions are not states of mind so much as movements of the mind ('emote' literally means 'move out');
and the mind is constantly changing. We do give some
intermittent direction to this perpetual shifting of emotions, but rarely to much purpose. If I become irritated,
I may resolve to be more patient, but I can't fix that
resolution. If I am not mindful, it is easily followed by
another decision: no more Mr Nice Guy. And if left to

itself this anger may well develop into fury, depending on what other conditions and associations become involved.

With the help of mindfulness, however, we can make emotions work for us more effectively. So, first catch your emotion. Not that we have to look for big strong emotions, although these might seem easiest to get a handle on. For most of us, big strong emotions are big crude ones, and big crude emotions hold us down. When emotions are strong, we are usually transfixed – with fear, or loathing, or desire. Strong emotions are reassuring because they give us harder ego-definition. A creative emotion, by contrast, includes the awareness that one's 'state' of mind is not a state but a movement. It is therefore, in a sense, more elusive; one's energies do not gather around it so readily.

To catch the more subtle emotions that are going on all the time, you have to sit very still and quiet, like a fisherman waiting for a bite. Look out for something physical to begin with – emotions experienced as sensations in the body, tension, or slumping. Gently releasing the knots, or straightening up, will release whatever emotion is held in your posture. Another way into emotion is through thought: catch passing thoughts, identify them, then reel in the quality of emotion that has triggered them. Sometimes you may have to sit for quite a while waiting for a pull on the line. Or just listen for emotions until they come to your attention like the sound of soft rain on the window. Sometimes becoming aware of emotions involves separating out a muddy confusion of them. Sometimes it means knowing that you are *not* feeling something. Is there something you don't want to notice or think about? Without worrying about what it might be, you can just become aware of that fenced-off area in your experience.

Whether you become aware of big, uncomfortable emotions – craving, despair, jealousy, anger – or subtle evanescent ones, or nothing much at all, is not really the point. You have already started the meditation, by coming back, again and again, to being receptive to yourself.

You may need to be patient if you find yourself in unfamiliar territory here. For many of us, strong emotions tend to exclude awareness of them. When I say 'I love you' or 'I hate you', I *am* that emotion. But in meditation you try to be aware of emotion even as you experience it, opening up a little space between yourself and the emotion. This gives you the freedom to recognize the emotion as your own, and become aware that you are not only separate from it but larger than it. You can learn to recognize the emotional tone of your experience just as you recognize the colours of things. Then you are in a position to halt the natural tendency to swing constantly between aware states of mind and unaware ones.

In dealing with a problem at work, for example, there are certain emotions that help the process: inspiration, enthusiasm, humour, interest, appreciation, contentment, devotion, commitment, belief. There is no need to name them to know that they are positive – you can *feel* they are. They are expansive, clear, energizing, directed, flexible, and imbued with awareness. Then there are emotions that block, drain, or fragment energy: resentment, hatred, boredom, anxiety, fear, guilt, craving, cynicism. Again, you know them by how they feel. They are cold, tight, closed off, rigid, alienating, unconscious; they aren't going anywhere except round in circles.

With this awareness it is possible to learn to disentangle the complex of emotions and consciously give them a particular direction. Emotions arise, like everything else, in dependence upon conditions. If you can learn which conditions give rise to positive emotions, you can consciously set up the right conditions – at least within yourself. External conditions are not always so much within our control, of course – although some of them are.

> *My heart in hiding*
> *Stirred for a bird, – the achieve of, the mastery of*
>   *the thing!*
> Gerard Manley Hopkins, 'The Windhover'

A mental state can always develop in a new direction. Confidence can be developed into faith or courage – or, if not nurtured, can degenerate into complacency. Left to itself, love may turn into clinging anxiety, and kindness may become sentimentality, but with awareness they can be developed into metta and compassion. Once we recognize the trajectories of the heart, we can learn to set their course towards a more conscious goal.

You can't insert emotion from outside, but you can locate and nurture whatever is in there, moving in the heart, quiet seeds of feeling behind any sense that life matters absolutely; tender buds of willingness behind any belief that you can make a daily difference to your own and others' deeper happiness. You can't force a seed to grow into a plant. All you can do – all you need do – is provide it with the right conditions. If you apply awareness, interest, persistence, and purpose – the seeds of metta will have the light, space, soil, and wall-trellis they need. The horticultural image is meant to encourage the traditional long-term vision and patience of the gardener. Another equally relevant quality is the kind of can-do assiduity needed to get a camp-fire going on a damp evening (the Buddha talks about rubbing two sticks together). These images – both of which are useful in their own way – reflect something very important. Buddhist practice is based on conditionality: set up the right conditions and it will work. There is no spooky magic about it. If it doesn't seem to be working, cast around for anything you may have overlooked in setting up those conditions.

The main thing is not to have a fixed idea of how metta will express itself. It is a protean faculty, emerging in all sorts of different forms depending on who or what it comes into contact with. When we see someone who is full of pain or hatred, our metta becomes compassion; when we see someone who is full of love, metta turns into joy and appreciation. And when we see a bird swooping and soaring, and our heart goes out to it in pleasure, that too is metta.

8

THE METTA BHAVANA

Who loves himself will never harm another.
The Udana

Joy is the mother of all the virtues.
Goethe

The following version of the Metta Bhavana is divided into five stages. You cultivate metta in the first stage towards yourself; in the second, towards a good friend; in the third, towards someone about whom you feel fairly indifferent; in the fourth, towards someone you dislike; finally, you allow your metta to spread out to encompass all human beings – indeed, all life – without exception.

There are many ways to set up the conditions for the arising of metta, and here I will suggest just a few of them. You may want to try out all the ideas mentioned, but in any given meditation session it makes sense to use just one or two of them. It would be nice to be able to say that it is 'simply' a matter of setting up conditions, but conditionality is never simple. You don't just put the nickel in the slot and get what you want. Awareness throws out all ready-made solutions. Meditation is never a repeat; it is always live. You are always addressing a different set of conditions – which of course means that you are never stuck with anything either.

THE FIRST STAGE

So you begin with yourself. A simple way to contact metta is just to say to yourself, 'May I be well, may I be happy.' Just drop these phrases into your consciousness and listen for an emotional echo, some kind of recognition from somewhere that you want to be happy. If you are sensitive enough, you may well pick up a wish to sabotage your own happiness as well. This is quite natural; in a sense it is what this meditation practice is designed to deal with. Finding metta for yourself does not necessarily involve feeling happy in any simple 'Thank God it's Friday' sort of way. You are introducing a friendly and supportive attitude to your own experience as if from the outside and seeing what happens.

You can try to see yourself as a good friend would see you, with affection. Watch yourself easing up, feel a softening around your eyes, in your jaw, shoulders, stomach. Or remind yourself of a time when you have been happy. Get back in touch with a feeling from the past – swimming lazily in the warm Mediterranean, say. Add a few details – the sky, the beach, the warmth, the lack of things to worry about – and recreate a feeling of serenity, of being composed and alive, a quiet bubbling of joy within a deep and spacious calm.

More simply, you can come back to the present and appreciate yourself at a gut level. Appreciate the miracle of sitting there being able to feel anything at all. Just enjoy having senses and look for any subtle pleasure there may be in your physical experience, any sense of poise, centredness, presence.

Or gather yourself around the heart, looking for a feeling of warmth there, perhaps a warm colour, red or gold, a sense of opening out, like a flower. Feel the flower in your heart, its petals glowing in the light of awareness, its roots drawing on energy from below. Or, if you respond more strongly to sound than to sight, you can experience metta as sound, as music.

It all sounds very nice, doesn't it? And sometimes it is. But this is not merely the feel-good bhavana – and sometimes it will not feel good. The aim is to develop a sense of warmth and caring towards yourself even if – as you become aware how you are feeling – you find that you are in some quite painful state of mind. In order to invoke an acceptance of happiness, you may also have to take in a knowledge of happiness lost. If one accepts the loss, one will be able to accept a deeper happiness. The wish to be happy is really the wish to be whole. Bear in mind that meditation is open-ended. Metta is not a mental state you get into; it is a movement, an emotional current. The active ingredient of metta is a quality of intent. This word 'intent' is interesting because it links the idea of intensity with a sense of purpose. So metta will often involve an intent to grow out of a comfortable state of mind into a deeper sense of your own welfare.

THE SECOND STAGE

In the second stage you fuel up with the friendliness you naturally feel anyway. Think about meeting up with a good friend. It works best to choose a friend for whom your feelings are quite straightforward – or as straightforward as feelings can ever be, anyway: not someone who elicits distracting emotions like lust, regret, grief, or maternal or paternal yearnings.

See your friend in your mind's eye – perhaps imagine them approaching, and the smile on their face – then notice the response to this in your heart, the feeling of being glad at the life of another person. Or simply conjure up a sense of being with your friend: their presence, the kind of energy they generate, their rhythms of speech, the tone of their voice, their laughter. Recall a good time you had together, and look for a certain quality of response in your heart, a steady relaxation, a welling up of joy, even of celebration.

Centre your awareness around that play of emotion, that emotional gesture of reaching out to touch another person. Perhaps imagine them in a situation where they would be happy, or imagine happiness blossoming in their heart, even visualizing a flower opening there. Then, having contacted your love for your friend, see if you can draw out that sense of active desire for their happiness. May they be well. May they be happy. May they be free from suffering.

THE THIRD STAGE

In the third stage you allow your friend to leave and bring to mind a person you know less well, someone towards whom you are to some degree indifferent, someone you see in two-dimensional terms. Perhaps this person performs a practical function in your life, like the postman, or merely features in the landscape of your life, a regular customer or fellow passenger on the journey to work.

The aim is to keep the flow of metta going. Even though you habitually feel less interest in and concern for this person, you deliberately open up to their basic desire to be happy. You may well feel yourself zoning out of this challenge. You don't have time in your life for this person. You have nothing in common. You wouldn't know what to say to them. The aim is to acknowledge that these limitations are accidental, not essential. Just for a few minutes, put that person at the centre of your attention. Practise separating the importance of a person from their importance to you.

This stage is the hinge on which the whole meditation turns, the point at which the weight of your appreciation and warmth for your friend can swing open a gate in your heart. It is a gate we are anxious to keep closed, because we define ourselves by setting limits. Feel that resistance in your restlessness and impatience to get back to your own concerns. Then imagine a smile on this person's face. Imagine them in a good place. As you make space for them, feel your heart becoming more spacious.

THE FOURTH STAGE

In the fourth stage you smuggle your metta behind enemy lines, or rather, you smuggle your enemy into the kindly realm of your metta. This is where the meditation starts to get a bit alchemical: in the fires of your hatred, anything soft-centred about your benevolence is burned away and real metta is forged. So some genuine animosity can get the sparks flying: strong emotion is a raw material, rich in energy, if you can put it through the refinery of your attentiveness and purpose.

But to save the whole practice from going up in smoke, it may be prudent, at least to begin with, to focus on someone who merely irritates you rather than the person who has ruined your life. You may even find that someone whom ordinarily you regard as a good friend is the best bet here – and including them in your meditation may help to resolve a current difficulty. It is generally a good idea not to think or worry too much about whom to choose for any of these stages. The important thing is to sustain the flow of metta so that you become practised in responding with kindness whenever you meet or think of anyone.

As with all the stages, keep it simple. Give yourself time to get used to your mind's tricks and tantrums. Think of meditation as a long-term thing. Relax your hands, your stomach, your hips, your shoulders, your jaw, your brows. Stay centred on your heart, and bring the 'enemy' as close as you can without letting your animosity lock in on them. Keep blowing away the storyline.

THE FIFTH STAGE

In this final stage, bring forward again the subjects of the first four stages – yourself, your friend, the 'neutral person', and the 'enemy'. Search out within your heart a response that does not distinguish between them, a recognition of the beauty of life wherever and however it blooms. Then start to explore more widely that quality of comprehensive engagement with the terror and the glory of being alive. Allow your metta to reach out and range over the whole world, hearing the quiet music of humanity echoing your own from every corner of the earth. The secret is in the details and the imagination. If only you observe people closely enough, try to enter their inner world, imagine their outer world, and see from where the choices they made originated, you cannot condemn or dismiss them.

Consider people of every different culture, living under all kinds of circumstances. Hear the voices of people speaking different languages. Look into their faces, into their eyes. Appreciate all sorts of totally individual lives, balking at no one. Whether you approve of them or not, whether they are rich or poor, villains or innocents, happy or suffering, you are trying to see everyone with the same eye for the irreplaceable jewel of life and the same desire for their happiness and freedom. Extend your metta not just to human beings, but to all living things. This world is our own, it is our own life, and every living thing, every beast in every land, every bird in the air, every fish in the ocean – is real and precious. You can even go imaginatively beyond the confines of this planet, to send warmth and good will to whatever beings there may be anywhere in this universe, or any universe.

This may suggest quite a busy practice, but you will find your own way to make these connections, always remembering that the focus should be in your heart centre. At the end of the meditation come back to sitting with yourself, absorbing and dwelling in that experience of expansiveness, and preparing to take your emotional awareness and friendly intent out of their controlled environment and back into the big bad world. Sometimes the meditation can seem dull or uncomfortable at the time, and sometimes its immediate effects on your daily life can be quite volatile, but you can gauge the success of the practice not so much by how it feels at the time as by the way your attitudes and actions towards others and the general temper of your mind change for the better.

9

FURTHER NOTES ON THE METTA BHAVANA

A sentimentalist is simply one who desires to have the luxury of an emotion without paying for it.
Oscar Wilde, in conversation

He is not affected by the reality of distress touching his heart, but by the showy resemblance of it striking his imagination. He pities the plumage, but forgets the dying bird.
Thomas Paine, of Edmund Burke, in *The Rights of Man*

André Malraux, the French writer and politician, describes, at the beginning of his *Antimemoires*, asking an old friend who has been a country priest for fifteen years what he has learned from listening to confessions. The priest replies that he has learned two things in the confessional: that people are much more unhappy than one imagines; and that grown-ups do not exist.

This is interesting not because it reveals that we are all sad children, but because it puts people in a completely different type of box from the one in which they usually like to appear, and the one in which we tend to put them. In the confessional we all become human and vulnerable. The Metta Bhavana does not offer penance or absolution, but it does go to the heart of what it is to be human. And there is no end to what can be said about it. In this section we will look at a few of the issues that may crop up as you begin to explore the meditation.

METTA FOR ONESELF

Almost all our feelings arise out of our relationships with others; almost all our emotions relate to others in one way or another. As a Buddhist one aims to realize this interconnection with others more deeply, but in order to do so one has to appreciate how radical our separation from one another really is. Conventionally, we may speak of, say, fifty thousand football supporters sharing the same feeling – whether 'gutted' or 'over the moon'. But by definition a feeling belongs to one person alone. A man suffering sympathetic labour pains is still experiencing his own pain. In our almost constant concern for our social identity we lose sight of the fact that the distinction between someone experienced as a self and someone experienced as another person is of a completely different order from the distinctions between people that we conventionally make.

This distinction can make the first stage of the Metta Bhavana seem rather convoluted. Being friendly towards yourself, like accepting yourself, sounds nice, but in practice it can seem impossibly circular. It can be reduced to something simpler, though: the awareness of your desire to be happy. This is the key to the whole practice. If we are in touch with our own desire to be happy, that is the first thing we see in others; no living being is then alien from our sympathies.

Curiously, however, the wish to be happy can be quite hard to connect with. This is because we want a bit more than to be happy – we want to *possess* happiness, earn it, marry it. We are either saving it for later – being dutiful, making money, dieting, that kind of thing; or we are grabbing it now – by being greedy or lazy – and regretting it later. In these ways we slowly become indifferent to our desire to be happy. At its most extreme, the desire to be happy becomes a desire not to be who we are. It gets lost inside a desire to be rich or good or secure. The result is that we operate from a very limited identity, leaving out of consideration the larger reality of existence.

In these attitudes towards ourselves we meet the attitudes that we have towards others – kindness, indifference, hatred, lack of awareness. The Metta Bhavana is incomplete without the first stage, and the first stage is developed fully only through the other stages. In our relations with others, we find out who we are. The Metta Bhavana is about engaging with a larger reality out there, embodied in what we think of as 'others', penetrating the barrier that the idea of 'others' represents. We are attached to others, we dismiss others, we condemn others, we ignore others – and we do the same to ourselves because we don't see the connection.

So, as with the rest of the practice, focusing on the positive is only the beginning. The aim of the Metta Bhanava is self-transformation, and we have to be careful how we think about this transformation. Buddhism makes no bones about using the language of eradication, even destruction: destruction of craving, unawareness, suffering. But this language can all too easily fuel the self-hatred that is, for many of us, at the top of the list of mental states to be 'eradicated'. Buddhism also uses the language of freeing ourselves from negative mental states but, again, this can easily turn into a kind of alienation. Metta isn't about manipulating our emotions, or ignoring negative emotions, or persuading ourselves that we are OK. We aren't saying, 'Just for a while, may I be the kind of nice person who deserves to be happy.'

These languages of destruction and freedom offer very challenging perspectives when we are ready for them. Another kind of language that Buddhism uses is that of compassion, very often embodied in the form of idealized Bodhisattvas. This language also has its danger, that of complacency, but it is probably the best language to start off with. From this perspective, real metta has to include the stuff we don't like to look at. We may say 'May I be well,' but the caring, sharing part of us that is going to get behind that sort of sentiment is not where our real energy is kept. Before we can say 'May I be well' with the whole of ourselves, we have to identify with the whole of ourselves. Metta for ourselves isn't just metta for the good bits; it has to include metta for the bits we aren't happy with – the enemy within. Developing metta for oneself has to start with being oneself, without illusions or pretence, without excuses or blame.

All of us, from time to time, receive kindness from others. Sometimes we have a sense of beneficence from nature as well. So we don't have to think of metta exclusively as something we try to nurture within ourselves. Instead, we can think of tuning in to it. No one 'possesses' metta. Rather than thinking of radiating lovingkindness as though we were its source, it may be more helpful to consider that we have somehow stopped it from getting through. When we are fully ourselves, metta is our natural response to the reality of beings. It is the most authentic response we can have. We don't put it on like a warm overcoat.

To contact metta, you may have to pick your way through some murky areas of your experience, but, all the time, watch for a glimmer of contentment, a flicker of energy, a gap of awareness, a pinpoint of faith, a momentary lightness, a broadening, an expansiveness, a pliancy, softness, warmth, clarity of heart. Even states of mind that are seemingly unhelpful to meditation usually offer something to work with. If you are sleepy, for example, you are also relaxed, perhaps calm, peaceful, even at ease. Somewhere in that state there will be a faint glow of awareness, and you can centre on that and slowly bring the light up. Or suppose you become aware of a knot of anxiety or anger. That knot also represents an energy source that you can make use of if you can turn down the mental volume.

Sometimes you can sit through an entire meditation session and, in the end, have the depressing feeling that you have got nowhere at all. But the fact that you have sat down and persisted with at least the idea of metta will have an effect, however muddy or distracted your state of mind might appear to be. Sometimes, after getting up from the cushion at the end of an apparently unproductive meditation session, one finds that – in response to meeting someone or seeing some interaction – one's heart is suddenly flooded with metta.

METTA FOR A FRIEND

When you move on to developing metta for a friend, there are two things that distinguish this process from a pleasant daydream. Firstly, just for once you are paying attention to the effect of the object of your attention upon your own state of mind. In a sense you are using your friend: using the natural positive feeling they call forth in you to fuel the development of a love that extends beyond your immediate circle, your friends and family, to a genuine caring for those many beings – the rest of the population of the planet – who are outside the magic circle of your habitual concern.

Secondly, you are giving a conscious direction to the process. Meditation is based on the fact that our essence is one of change. It is concerned with being aware how we change, and redirecting that process of change. To develop metta for your friend you have to let go of any claims or demands on them. You wish them well for their sake, not yours. It is good to imagine your friend bathing in the nice warm glow that you are radiating, but it is important not to see them as somehow dependent on your radiant goodwill.

This is a good time to establish the hard-headed, unsentimental aspect of metta. A friend is not simply someone who gives you a good feeling, but someone you look out for, and this is an important aspect of metta that needs to be carried into the rest of the meditation: a sense that doing this meditation is going to change the way you live.

METTA FOR A STRANGER

When we leave a friend and bump into someone we know less well, we usually find ourselves responding quite warmly to this new person. A stranger may be treated to the smile still in our eyes from our meeting with our friend. In the third stage of the Metta Bhavana you do this consciously. Not allowing the warmth to disperse, you sustain your concentration on your feeling for your friend, and in doing so you get a sense of what it would be like to care about this other, more 'neutral' person. You are not necessarily going to be taking your relationship with them beyond its present limits, but you are trying to distinguish practical limitations from emotional brick walls.

The power of good films and novels is that they introduce us to individuals we will never know and make us care about them. They do this by focusing on the intricate interlocking of day-to-day details that on their own amount to very little, but which together add up to the kind of unique patterning we call humanity. Use your imagination to build up elements of that patterning out of whatever details you notice about this person. Their hopes and fears and anxieties are different from ours, but we can be sure that they have them, and that they feel as real to them as ours to us.

With imagination we can see everyone we meet in this way. If we notice the way we look at people in the street, it is usually possible to catch ourselves making semi-conscious snap judgements: 'attractive', 'rich', 'shallow', 'scrounger'. We can dismiss someone in an instant, not seeing where they have come from or where they are going – or rather, not seeing that we have no idea where they have come from or where they are going. So it is much more enjoyable and interesting to find the streets filling up with these mysterious individuals. Try to allow the neutral person to be free of your projections, your habitual ways of categorizing people. Let them go their own way, be themselves, unique just as you are.

Take care to stay focused on the emotion of metta. You will want to use your imagination to help you connect with that person, but the meditation should not involve visualizing endless scenarios. You conjure up a particular image for one reason: to intensify and direct the flow of your positive emotion.

METTA FOR AN ENEMY

Here we bring love and hatred together into the ring – but the idea is not that the one should steamroller the other and the worthy winner take all. Sometimes we find it hard to admit, even to ourselves, that there are people we dislike, let alone people we would think of as enemies. But if we are honest with ourselves we will discover that we do dislike some people. It is common to feel animosity towards some tyrant or oppressor, but it is usually more productive in this stage of the Metta Bhavana to focus on someone closer to home.

If you can be honest about how you feel towards someone, anger can sometimes even be turned into something approaching affection. This calls for a certain courage and big-heartedness. Hatred is a kind of attachment, and we like to have someone or something upon whom or which to vent our discomfort or pain. I have every right to be bitter, we cry. If we unhook that attachment, we are left with that uncomfortable feeling, even that pain, but at least that person is no longer pulling our emotional strings. Sometimes, of course, we hate someone because we have not forgiven ourselves. It may be helpful, if uncomfortable, to look for something we have not acknowledged, for which we want to be forgiven.

If you stand for anything you will sometimes have to stand up against individuals who oppose your values. Keeping quiet, trying to be understanding, even being friendly, is not necessarily an expression of metta, but if you are feeling metta, you will be able to deal with people you dislike without hatred and without being false or evasive.

If you run into problems in this stage, try loosening up physically, whilst staying centred on the momentum of goodwill you have built up. Bear in mind that the positivity you experience will be a constantly changing complex of emotions, fading out sometimes, then coming back in a slightly different mix. What you are looking for is flexibility, an ability to see beyond your limited, narrow view of the person you dislike, and break out of the mental rat-run you slip into whenever their name comes up. They want what you want from life: to be happy and to be free from pain. They are going to die one day, just as you are. You can let them be more than the villain in your little drama, let them be themselves.

UNIVERSAL METTA

A lot of people live on this planet, and there is a danger in this stage, if you are adept at visualizing, of churning out a kind of airline commercial, with ethnic characters from around the world waving up at you in your love-jet as you cruise at thirty thousand feet. But all this should actually be taking place just under the ribs. We know we live in one world, but do we feel it? How much is it going to cost us if we do start to feel it? Look for a feeling of expansiveness, of release from a sense of reality that is centred on yourself. Surprisingly, caring about more people does not multiply one's anxieties, indeed, it tends to loosen the knots.

Metta does not occur on its own; it comes into being in dependence on all sorts of other qualities. You aren't trying to squeeze love or friendliness out of yourself like toothpaste. You are trying to be aware of yourself and others – aware of your fear of caring too much, and also aware that your capacity to care can grow bigger. You will radiate metta when you have set up the conditions in which it can happen. Metta is cultivated not just by being positive and friendly but, more crucially, by being aware of that response, how it develops and how it fails to develop.

PART FOUR

TAKING MEDITATION FURTHER

10

DISTRACTIONS

To be able to do one thing at a time is the whole art of life.
Sangharakshita, *Peace is a Fire*

What isn't part of ourselves doesn't disturb us.
Hermann Hesse, *Demian*

When you are learning to meditate, it probably won't be long before you come to a conclusion that stops you in your tracks. You can't meditate, you may decide, because you get so distracted. But to become aware of the distractions is to begin to understand the whole process of meditating.

Whatever we try to do, we are going to experience our mind. We can't magically experience another, better mind. We get distracted from the meditation because we are not content to experience who we are, the person we have chosen to be. That is, we get distracted because we are not prepared to engage with that state of mind, see it for what it is, and start turning it into a conscious activity, rather than simply an experience.

As soon as we name these distractions or hindrances, we start to create a different kind of mind, and sometimes that is all we have to do to shake them off. The Buddhist tradition offers a list of five basic ingredients, one or more of which will comprise our distractions. These are: craving for sense-objects, ill will, restlessness and anxiety, mental or physical dullness, and doubt (in the sense of an undermining scepticism).

These distractions represent our stock responses to life, and they constantly find events or things or people to hook on to. The same situation – the train not arriving on time, say – may provoke anxiety in me, anger in a man standing next to me, a dull weariness in a woman slumped on a bench further down the platform, a kind of escapist craving in someone beside the confectionery dispenser, and cynicism in yet another passenger reading a newspaper. The lateness of the train may seem, to each of us on the platform, to be responsible for these emotions, but it is really no more than the vehicle by which a residual emotional attitude has come to our attention. If the train had arrived on time, quite probably some other aspect of our journey would have prompted the arrival of whatever negative mental state was hovering around us.

WHERE DO DISTRACTIONS COME FROM?

Distractions are essentially unconscious; they contain no space for awareness. They seem to arise from nowhere and take over as though we had been secretly invaded. When we start meditating we have to keep the hindrances at bay while we build a bridgehead of awareness. We are then in a position to persuade them to come out slowly with their hands in the air.

Relaxed concentration inevitably brings hindrances out of the woodwork, and this allows us to own them and decide what to do with them. To take a very obvious example, if we have an itch we usually scratch it automatically, but in meditation we become aware of the itch and also aware that we can choose whether to scratch it or not. The mind also has its itches. The aim of meditation is to bring every movement of the mind or body into the realm of consciousness, and thus of choice, and thus of freedom.

We are making choices all the time, mostly in an unconscious and habitual way, and experiencing the results of those choices, which are also more or less unconscious. One finds oneself opening the fridge, or picking up a book, or lighting a cigarette, or getting into a rage, or looking in a shop window, or losing heart, as one's emotional energy directs.

Meditation interrupts this process by reducing the volume of sensory objects coming to our attention. The mind continues to come up with distracting objects, but it gradually becomes obvious that at some level we have chosen them ourselves. The real obstacle to meditation (and indeed to anything else) is not that we have something to worry about, or that someone has been unkind to us, or that there is noise going on outside, or that we have an itch, or that we have something or someone very fascinating to think about, or that we can't really be sure that what we are doing isn't a waste of time. What gets in the way is that we unconsciously lose our initiative to such circumstances, and let them determine our state of mind and our whole life.

We are under the spell of the hindrances. They are pointless and sometimes painful, but they are there, unbidden. Their nature is to undermine what we are doing, whether in meditation or out of it, with conflicting thoughts, impulses, and volitions. They undermine our ability to act with integrity and wholeheartedness, but they are what they are only because they are unconscious – that is their only power. So the real work of meditation is not so much a matter of concentrating on an object as monitoring and managing the flow of mental states that emerges out of this exercise, and that either supports or undermines it.

MINDING THE HINDRANCES

We want to unify our energies, and to do this we need to resolve our inner conflicts. These conflicts are 'inner' because we have to hold back parts of ourselves. (If we didn't, we would probably get ourselves locked up.) If we hold back too much, we eventually pay a heavy price. We tend to lose touch with the sources of our energy, and this results in resentment, lassitude, craving, anxiety, and doubt – yes, the hindrances.

Given that these are all expressions of conflict, you don't want to get into conflict with them. Instead, try to broaden your awareness of yourself to include other aspects as well; bring warmth and even humour into the picture. The trouble with hindrances is that they think they are the only onion in the soup and that they are going to stay that way. In fact, a hindrance is sometimes sitting on top of its opposite. Love, energy, stillness, and faith are not always comfortable states of mind, and when they are beginning to emerge, sometimes only anger, dullness, anxiety, and indecision will keep them down. So it is worth focusing particularly on whatever positive quality the hindrance may be trying to hide.

Remind yourself too that hindrances are not states of mind (as they imagine themselves to be) but movements of mind. They are moving on. If your overall mental state is fairly steady, you can just watch them pass over the sky of your mind like fluffy white clouds. That is, you encourage what is called a 'sky-like mind' or, as it is sometimes known nowadays, 'teflon mind' or 'non-stick consciousness'.

But what if they are not so fluffy? It is useful to classify hindrances in the traditional way, usually as one of the big five, because the more generalizing we can be about them, the more easily we can distance ourselves from the personal details that draw us into them. But the reality is that they are a mix: they each depend on the support of the others. Some are simply working at much more deeply unconscious levels than others. Dullness, say, may be the most obvious characteristic of your current mental state, but you may be sure that others – frustration, resentment, craving, lack of self-belief – are in the background, producing quite an individual, personal kind of dullness that tends to come back again and again.

If, instead of experiencing occasional fluffy clouds, you experience only occasional patches of clear blue sky, you could switch metaphors and identify your regular visitors as clamouring children, each with their own tone of voice – preachy, sulky, panicky, needy, dreamy, smart-alecky, piggy, fussy, and so forth. Sometimes you may need to take control and consider what these apparently harmless children might grow into, that is, you need to take an active interest in the progeny of your own mind. It might seem as if thoughts and feelings come and go with no harm done; but a little reflection makes it obvious that they pull our strings, and we dance to their silent cacophony. Bringing more awareness to these parts of yourself, rather than letting them run around like delinquents, will make the energy tied up in them available to you. Furthermore, if you can be an adult to your own negative mental states, you can also be an adult to the negative mental states of others. Real kindness comes not from a nice warm feeling, but from having the strength and humility to put your own feelings to one side when they get in the way.

While it is being cleared, a river will become muddy from disturbed sediment. It's the same with meditation. The process of becoming aware may make things more chaotic in the short term. Meanwhile, it is always a good idea to come back to your physical experience, relaxing and straightening your posture, in order to re-establish an essential, authentic basis of self-awareness. Hindrances can often be dealt with on the physical level. When you are distracted, come back to the straightforward authenticity of your physical experience: softening, relaxing, waking up, straightening, broadening, opening.

UNHOOKING THE HINDRANCES

Sometimes a persistent hindrance may have something to say that is worth hearing, and, if we listen, it will begin to speak to us more clearly. Our distractions sometimes carry – in their tone if not in their content – important messages. They may be the means whereby our emotions, which do not always have a direct line to our awareness, bring themselves to our attention. Alternatively, a hindrance may be our way of protecting ourselves from something. When the mind wanders off, that may be an unconscious strategy for maintaining a superficial level of awareness when we do not have the emotional resources to deal with exposure to a deeper reality.

With all the hindrances, the trick is to avoid letting them hook on to anything, or to find a way of unhooking them. To do that, we need to find out what it is that they have hooked themselves on to. It sometimes helps to think of the hindrances as creative qualities that have become entranced with the surface of our experience, like Narcissus falling in love with his own reflection, instead of looking beyond into the depths of the water below. For example, desire can be a very positive thing – whether as a healthy appetite or a noble aspiration. But desire can hook itself on to something and get stuck – we can't shift our desire past our craving for a cigarette, say. This is what happens to the hero of the fairy story who is given three wishes – getting stuck on limited desires, he fritters his wishes away.

It's similar with aversion. In the Greek myth of Perseus and Medusa, anyone who looks directly at the monstrous Medusa is turned to stone; but the hero Perseus approaches her by watching her reflection in his shield, then cuts off her head. Our aversion, too, gets stuck on external obstacles: a person, thing, or situation seems to bring it into being. But our *bêtes noires* must be approached as reflected images if we want to retain our freedom around them.

The other hindrances can also alert us to the possibility of going deeper. If we notice that our energy is stuck in fidgeting, we can free it so that it can take us to deeper levels of concentration. As we become still, the energy of restlessness persists; it has become the pulley (the poet George Herbert's image) by which we have escaped the warm, grey fug of superficial contentment.

Similarly, loosening the grip of our anxiety may allow us to explore our deeper fears and open up to the vast expanse of the reality in which we feel so insecure. As for our tendency to nod off in order to resist our experience, this can become an ability to put aside our difficulties and allow space for healing to happen in its own time and at its own level. And the fifth hindrance, doubt and indecision, can be made use of as well. If we can direct it instead of being its victim, we can learn a lot from questioning the assumptions that underlie all the hindrances, including doubt and indecision itself.

WHEN NOTHING SEEMS TO WORK

If distractions are creating havoc in your mind, and if over time the meditation practice doesn't seem to be settling them down, you probably need to take a closer look at the conditions that have produced this state of affairs. Do you attempt to be mindful or aware outside your meditation practice? If not, perhaps the meditation on its own is not enough to deal with the backlog of unconscious impressions and reactions. Do you need to be a bit more sensitive and responsive, or are you, on the contrary, too slack or vague? Have you taken up meditation very dutifully, so that you are keeping too tight a rein on the practice? Are you afraid something terrible will happen to you if you stop? (It won't.) Or is there some aspect of your life about which you feel uncomfortable? Meditation should make you more sensitive to the ethics of what you do, and one way of not having to look at your ethics is to keep your meditation superficial.

You may also need to pay more attention to noticing how you feel about the meditation. Do you really want to see through your distractions, or do you, deep down, have a sense that what they are talking about is too important and interesting to dispense with?

The hindrances give us vital clues to our fundamental attitudes about what is possible for us. Do we see a clear and happy state of mind as a natural human condition that is accessible to us, or do we put limits on how clear and happy we can be? Do we think our mental state is a solid fact we're stuck with, or do we see our state of mind as essentially fluid, the product of a constantly fluctuating complex of conditions that we can change? What limits to growth do we set ourselves? Where have we put the glass ceiling? Do we take seriously the Buddhist conception of limitless potential to transform our consciousness? And if we do, are we perhaps afraid of the responsibility that this throws on us?

FAITH IN MEDITATION

Who would have thought my shrivelled heart
Could have recovered greenness? It was gone
Quite underground; as flowers depart
To see their mother root, when they have blown.
George Herbert, 'The Flower'

Being able to concentrate in meditation is not about being able to apply ourselves to something dull. It is about finding things – finding life – rich and complex and deeply satisfying. We say 'My mind wanders,' but what that means is that only part of the mind is engaging itself – and rather a small, shrivelled part at that. Meditation is subject to the same habits that govern the rest of our lives: we may end up doing it because we are afraid of the consequences of not doing it, or because we want approval, or because it's our job, or because we have always done it, or because we hope to get something for nothing from it. Meanwhile, our enthusiasm, our commitment, our joy, waits for some deeper meaning to arrive.

When you first learn to meditate, it has its own significance. It is something you do for its own sake. Later on, you might do it in the same way you snatch breakfast in the morning. It's a utilitarian thing, a means to an end. It is natural to come to experience meditation in this way – how your day goes depends on your meditation, and vice versa – but while you are doing it you do need to allow it to have its own significance. It isn't just something you get out of the way so that you can get on with something more important. It's like having a good dinner: you need its energy in order to do other things, but you still need to enjoy the food for its own sake if you want to digest it properly.

Because it is something you do on your own, it is easy to forget that the significance of meditation lies not only in its effect upon you. Whether implicitly or explicitly, you are meditating for the sake of others; and it helps to remind yourself of the wider patterns created by your efforts and intentions. A simple way to do this is to try a devotional practice. Staying in touch with the significance of meditation will help you through the times when you don't seem to be benefiting from it. Sometimes you just have to nourish the roots, keep coming back to the practice, and wait for spring to arrive.

11

BALANCED EFFORT

You can't beat hens to make them lay.
Marianne Moore, 'The Student'

It isn't possible to have a meditation practice without the discipline to work at it regularly, whether you feel like it or not. The idea of any practice, whether it's musical, artistic, sporting, intellectual, or meditative, is to impose something on yourself, and demand something of yourself, not for money or fun, but for the joy and the love of it. Meditation gives you the momentum to take you through your present difficulties, and when it is going well, a commitment develops that will see you through. However, when the going gets tough, you will often find that trying harder doesn't work. When meditation seems really hard, even painful, you may knit your brows, clench your brain, and try to accelerate past all the unnecessary feelings and mental processes that get in the way of what you think the experience should be like, but somehow you get no closer to that experience.

On the other hand, not making an effort doesn't seem to work either. If you don't make any effort, you drift and become vague about what exactly you are doing. In the end you don't really see the point of meditating at all.

To begin with, it can be a huge effort just to sit still for ten minutes and keep returning your attention to the focus of the meditation. But you have to relax that effort each time before you try again. It's like learning to drive a car. To get into gear you need to push down the clutch pedal, but to get going you need to release it again: the process is an engagement followed by a letting go. This becomes a smooth manoeuvre when you're used to it, but while you're still learning, the car is going to judder and jerk. Similarly, although depth in meditation comes through engaging more and more of your energy, this is not achieved by making more and more effort. Effort is necessary at first, but the next step is to reduce the effort.

What you're aiming for is a bit of a stretch, without being grabby. Less is more – and more difficult. You need to make just enough effort to enable you to attend to what is going on at this moment. Any more means that you are reaching out to experience something else; and if you do that, you will miss the present moment altogether. The harder you concentrate, the less you are aware.

We want results, and if possible a short cut to those results. Ideally we'd like to make the effort, get the results, and relax. But the kind of effort you need is the kind of effort required to listen to your child when you have a hundred and one things to do by last Tuesday. However important the things on your to-do list, it is almost always more important to listen to that message from the present, trivial as it may seem.

Effort in meditation is not 'an' effort. There is no point at which you stop making it. It is as little effort as is required, sustained as fully you can manage. It is a continuity of effort – that is, it has to be combined with mindfulness. It's like covering a statue in gold leaf. The whole thing has to be covered, but too thick a covering will destroy its definition. At no point on the surface will you find more than the finest layer of gold – yet the effect is to transform the image. The result of this balancing of gentle effort with mindfulness is perseverance.

I present this key element in meditation in this way because, for many people, making more effort is the easy option. It requires no imagination or awareness. Balanced effort is effort balanced with other qualities, and it has to be kept in the background to allow the shyer qualities through. In judo – to take a classic example – it may seem as if all you need do is make a bit more effort, and your opponent will fall over. If he is small enough this may well happen, but in the long run, making more effort is going to get in the way of learning how to put down even the strongest opponents – getting your grip right, breaking their balance, timing, stepping, turning, pulling, and so on. Once everything is in place, you can bring to bear against the big guy a huge effort that is not willed effort, not just a call for exertion from 'head office', but rooted effort, effort that is embodied, that explodes from the earth, through the toes, right up to the fingertips.

The Buddha likened balanced effort to tuning a stringed instrument. The strings, he said, should be neither too slack nor too tight. Another way of putting this is to say that the right kind of effort has been achieved when the whole body of the instrument vibrates. Indeed, one of the great judo champions of recent years, Robert van de Walle, who was well-known for the powerful physicality of his judo, enjoyed a notable come-back late in his career, after his English trainer made him sing as part of his training.

If your practice is lazy, dull, and uninspired, more effort alone won't work. Meditation engages us in something that runs counter to our normal interests. For it to be effective, we have to leave behind our desire for sense experience, and to do that we have to feel a real dissatisfaction with that ordinary mental state together with a real interest in developing something else. The only way to do this is to believe that there *is* something else. Whether you were aware of it or not, this faith got you meditating in the first place; you might as well continue to use it. Instead of pushing yourself to meditate, find something to pull you. If you bring faith in the possibility of change into contact with your perseverance, you will develop an unshakeable determination that will take you as far as you want. To begin with, you will have to keep hauling your attention out of a rut, but after a while your concentration will be rolling and you just have to keep the tow-rope taut.

Once your concentration is established, you can move in on the object of your meditation, make closer contact with it, look for a clearer definition. Then relax, loosen up, broaden the field of your awareness. If you become distracted or a bit dull and woolly, focus on the object again. Gradually, as your energy becomes more concentrated, this adjustment will become more subtle. The aim is a steady accumulation of energy, gradually bringing all your resources to bear upon the object, whilst maintaining your awareness.

Outside meditation you may need to put in rather more effort to remain aware, because you will have rather more than your own mental states to be aware of. On starts meditation thinking it will sort out one's head. What one finds, however, is that this involves sorting out the heart as well, and that this means moving on from oneself to become more aware of others. And people can be more work (as well as fun) in the flesh than in the freeze-frame of meditation. There is a whole genre of stories about monks or hermits emerging into the world after years of meditation and proceeding to make complete asses of themselves.

12

CONCENTRATION

That blessed mood ...
In which the burthen of the mystery,
In which the heavy and the weary weight
Of all this unintelligible world,
Is lightened: – that serene and blessed mood,
In which the affections gently lead us on, –
Until, the breath of this corporeal frame
And even the motion of our human blood
Almost suspended, we are laid asleep
In body, and become a living soul:
While with an eye made quiet by the power
Of harmony, and the deep power of joy,
We see into the life of things.
  Wordsworth, 'Tintern Abbey'

I may not hope from outward forms to win
The passion and the life, whose fountains are within.
  S.T. Coleridge, 'Dejection, an Ode'

There are all kinds of situations in which we need to concentrate, but we usually get concentrated by excluding parts of ourselves from our awareness – often our body and our emotions – in order to complete the task in hand. In this way our energies are divided – parts of us are elsewhere, making themselves known only in the form of hindrances – and we experience more or less unconscious conflict. In meditation, however, we welcome these conflicting parts of ourselves into our awareness, with the result that we eventually become truly concentrated and harmonized. This harmonized condition of being is self-created. We are no longer trying to wring satisfaction out of the world by plugging into sense experience; we have our own generator. The result of this is that we experience great joy.

As you sit to meditate, look for the joy that comes from being very clear about and intensely interested in what you are doing. You may notice resistance to this, a subtle sense of withdrawal and disconnection, or a sense of grabbiness or overshooting. This is distraction working at a more refined level. Engaging in a process that takes us beyond the orbit of the small self with its anxieties and vanities, we have a natural fear of releasing too much energy and an equally natural desire to appropriate the whole experience.

One way of thinking about this sort of resistance to progress is in terms of Mara. According to Buddhist mythology, Mara is the ruler of the mundane world. It was Mara's daughters who attempted to distract the Buddha from the meditation that culminated in his

Enlightenment, and Mara's sons who were said to have attacked the Buddha to prevent his gaining Enlightenment (their missiles turned into flowers). So Mara finds any sign that someone is attempting to leave his realm, the realm of mundane experience (and this is essentially what one is doing in meditation) very threatening, and he throws distractions in their path to block their escape. Distractions can thus be seen as signs that we have dug deeply enough to stir him up. Mara has no real power: in fact, to become aware of his presence, and recognize him for who he is, is enough to disempower him. Another way of looking at what is happening is that the space you create by sitting still has a tendency to act like a kind of vacuum, drawing up into consciousness whatever dubious states of mind are lurking below the surface. But with steady effort, it is as if the pressure gradually becomes equalized, and the mind starts to inhabit the open space of your meditation as its natural environment, where it can move freely.

If you manage to sustain a sense of contentment and enthusiasm, at some point you will notice that you have left behind any sense of distraction or resistance. You begin to experience the natural results of being happy, fulfilled, and content, free from inner conflict. You still have to keep setting up the conditions for a deeper concentration. You continue to give your attention to what is present before you rather than what you would like to be there. But you become very still. It is as if the stillness soaks through your body and mind until your whole being brims with quietness. As that peace spills over into pleasure, you may get a bit grabby or fearful, and the concentration may slip away. When this happens, you can just smile and make another approach.

Sooner or later you may find yourself suffused with a tangible yet subtle physical pleasure, an intense comfort and clarity of body and mind. As you maintain a delicate but totally continuous contact with the object of concentration, this focus will be haloed by a warm and clear awareness of thoughts and feelings. Any emotional knots you encounter will no longer have the power to distract you. Your thoughts will be pliant and responsive, and you will be able to direct them without arousing resistance or distraction or dullness. Your reflections will have an emotional warmth to them, and a brightness, as if they come mounted on velvet. Or you become like an eagle – totally focused, watchful, but at the same time floating pleasurably on upward currents of emotional warmth.

This state of mind is the first stage of concentration, the first of four *dhyanas*, as they are called. It can be a surprise at first that such a state of mind is freely available, once you can contain your emotional energy instead of being stuck in it. But once you have experienced dhyana, you begin to become more sensitive – in everyday life as well as in meditation – to how you can cultivate this freeing up of your mental states. A crucial factor in the development of meditative concentration is pleasure. The quality of the positive feeling develops and becomes more refined as the concentration deepens, but it is always there: concentration and pleasure, even bliss, arise in dependence upon each other.

In the second dhyana, you are filled with delight and rapture, and experience a tremendous movement of energy in the subtle experience of your body, particularly as emotional blocks are released. You may no longer need the support of the meditation technique; you just keep directing attention towards certain qualities or tendencies in your experience, especially attending to any feelings of pleasure in your body.

Gradually you become so absorbed in, even transported by, that welling up of rapture – experiences of tingling and intense but subtle vibration – that you stop reflecting upon your experience. You are aware of what is happening, but your experience is not on an everyday, conceptual level; it is more visionary. You may not literally experience visions, heavenly music, or divine messages, but this is the level on which such experiences can occur. You may experience temperature changes and, more typically, your body may shake and shiver. The aim is to contain this energy, and to sit as still as possible without actually suppressing the energy.

With the arising of the third dhyana, having allowed rapture to fill you and having experienced the bliss of that fulfilment, you feel the rapture fade away to leave a deeper, more purely mental bliss. It is as if that bliss is hidden in the rapture, just as the rapture was hidden in the concentration of the first dhyana, and as all the joys of the dhyanas are hidden in the messy everyday mind. This is simply to say that we all have this hidden potential, and that it is the business of meditation to uncover it. In the third dhyana you experience scarcely any separation from the rest of life. Integrated within, you are connected to a greater reality.

As absorption deepens further, the feeling becomes more and more refined until you are absolutely still. This is the fourth dhyana, and it takes one outside the categories in which one usually experiences the world (like 'mind' and 'matter'). It is therefore from this ultimate state of human integration that supernormal powers develop.

The higher dhyanas (and there are more even beyond the fourth dhyana) represent very rarefied states of consciousness indeed. But the first dhyana is within easy reach; in fact, you don't have to be sitting in meditation to experience it. Even the second dhyana is sometimes experienced – particularly in connection with the fine arts – by people who have never concerned themselves with meditation as such. By the same token, you can support the arising of dhyana wherever you can bring a limpid intimacy of attention to things, the kind of subtle vibrancy of perception which is perhaps more easily accessed in our response to music, art, and so on.

13

INSIGHT MEDITATION

Meanwhile the mind, from pleasure less,
Withdraws into its happiness; –
The mind, that ocean where each kind
Does straight its own resemblance find; –
Yet it creates, transcending these,
Far other worlds, and other seas;
Annihilating all that's made
To a green thought in a green shade.
   Andrew Marvell, 'The Garden'

If you do not expect the unexpected, you will never find
it.
   Heraclitus

Meditation is a means of developing our natural capacity for joy and love. But how far can we take it? On what
does this capacity of ours depend? What happens when
our world falls apart, when people close to us die when

they aren't supposed to, when we grow old or helpless before we're ready? Underneath our joy and love, what waits for us? What do we do with the aspects of our experience that are not touched by joy and love: fear and grief and rage and humiliation? The refined, positive states of mind we develop in meditation are not ends in themselves. Our new-found serenity must be tempered by a meeting with the real facts of life.

These facts are what we are most afraid of, and our lives are built around their avoidance, but according to Buddhism we suffer not because we cannot avoid them but because our whole being is committed to trying to avoid them – trying to avoid aspects of life that, ultimately, are unavoidable. In the end, we are not in control. Buddhism is basically concerned, through the practice of ethics and meditation, with loosening up the self-protective habits of the mind, the wonderful evolutionary adaptations we have all inherited from millions of years of trying to control our environment. The idea is to allow something to emerge, or to awaken, that is not part of that mechanism for controlling our experience that we call the self. This something is called vipassana, or insight, even transcendental insight – 'transcendental' because it transcends one's previously limited perspective. It is the awakening mind, or big mind. When it emerges, we are no longer totally identified with the self or terrified of its inevitable demise, and we are free from having to cater to its impossible demands. A burden is dropped.

This sounds great, but anyone who has had a glimpse of awakening before they are ready will testify that it is also unbearable. And in some sense the converse applies: what is unbearable is of the same nature as awakening.

Insight is the nature of reality coming right down to earth and breaking in upon our cosy delusion. The nature of reality makes an appearance in any experience of failure or loss or humiliation. It is there whenever our sense of ourselves cracks open, whenever we feel exposed or wronged or grief-stricken. A cherished plan fails, a lover walks out, a letter brings terrible news, and the cold shock of reality shakes us, for a while, into being more real. And – perhaps this is even harder for us to take – sometimes beauty or joy or love shakes us to the core too; it can pierce us to the heart in a way that is almost physically painful. One can also say that there is an element of insight in the strange sense of liberation and happiness that sometimes arises within a context of painful loss. As the travel writer Freya Stark writes in her autobiography, 'The beckoning counts, and not the clicking of a latch behind you.'

When someone who is part of our life dies, we have the sense of some deep root being broken, and this experience is the closest most of us come to real insight. Witnessing a death, we experience the nuts and bolts of being human. Death is very ordinary. It is a humdrum business with all sorts of practical details to be attended to. The clocks don't stop – life goes on. And in some sense insight involves the coming together of these two things – ordinary life and ordinary death, because it is fundamental to our delusion that we leave death out of our experience of life.

In fact, insights call out to us every day, but we don't usually hear them because they challenge us, they reverberate with implications for how we should live. An insight is essentially a recognition, an acknowledgement of some truth. It stops being an insight when we find a way of separating that recognition from how we go about our life. To take a simple example, we may see very clearly that there is no justification for the existence of industrial abattoirs just to provide our taste pleasures, but we cannot resist that bacon sandwich, because understanding is not the same as insight. Likewise, the experience of someone close to us dying only turns into an insight to the extent that it changes the way we live. The insight or realization may not come to us at the time. It is more likely to dawn later. Like Wordsworth's definition of poetry, it arises from 'emotion recollected in tranquillity'.

Meditation as a process of integration is important to insight because it interrupts our normal way of processing our experience. The way we usually learn is by adding more and more material, as if the mind were an enormous filing cabinet. Being able to compartmentalize our experience in this way is a useful (and perhaps particularly masculine) accomplishment: it enables us to do things half-consciously, and so allows us to do things we don't feel like doing, but it does make it difficult for a complete shift in our being to take place. One reason books that promise to 'change your life' don't generally do so is that our unconscious response is to open a new file labelled 'life-changing experiences'.

Buddhist meditation gradually replaces this filing cabinet with a living relationship to our experience. 'Having experiences' becomes a constant reconfiguring of the relationship between the self and the world. If our attitude is one of consuming experience, there is only going to be room for our experience to come to us in the form of a verbal report for immediate filing. The only way truly to experience anything is to be changed by it – or rather, in it. To experience metta or compassion is to listen to what it says about our way of living.

We originally overcame our fear of the world by knowing it and naming it, but through this knowing we now hold the world at arm's length. By knowing our way around the world, by knowing exactly what is going on, we allay our anxiety, but we also feed it, because underneath there is a growing uneasiness at our ignorance about what is *really* going on. In meditation we start unknowing things – that is, we make our experience conscious rather than unconsciously filing it away – and begin to gain access to a deeper knowledge.

The Metta Bhavana and the Mindfulness of Breathing prepare us for insight to arise by quietly and steadily undermining fixed ideas and rigid emotional attitudes, so that we may sustain and accept the ultimate deconstruction of our experience of reality rather than being overwhelmed by it. Any meditation can bring home to us certain radical insights, and even, if we add a reflective element to it, contain the possibility of transcendental insight. Impermanence can be realized by just watching the breath come and go.

However, there is a particular class of Buddhist meditation, called insight meditation, which is specifically concerned with the contemplation or interrogation of reality. It comes in all sorts of forms, some simple, some weird and wonderful. The general principle is that one contemplates something – whether cognitive, perceptual, or symbolic – designed to trigger insight. You can contemplate reality in the form of a symbolic visual image together with a mantra. You can turn over in your mind a Zen koan, a type of question to which there can be no rational reply. Or you can minutely examine your mental states and observe how they arise in dependence upon one another, and how none of them has any independent existence.

The practice of insight begins with unremitting reflections on the most fundamental existential questions. These reflections are sustained until they gradually begin to colour or flavour one's whole experience of life. Then, in meditation, one contemplates this developing sense of the way things are, bringing to that contemplation all the qualities one has developed through one's meditation practice: a fully integrated mind, steady, expansive, and untroubled by any discomfort of mind or body.

All this prepares us for insight – but we can't summon it up deliberately. The term Buddha means 'one who is awake' – but the dreaming mind can only dream; it is the awakening mind that awakens. In the end, we will awaken to reality not by telling ourselves what is real, or how reality works, but by being more real. Beyond having ideas about reality – in a scientific, philosophical, or religious sense – we must prepare to meet it at every moment, both in meditation and out of it. We prepare to meet it by the constancy and kindness of our attentiveness, not allowing any part of our life to hide away from our meditation practice, and not allowing our practice to ring-fence any other part of our lives.

We prepare the ground by reminding ourselves that we are dreaming, and by being a bit clearer and more aware about the way we ordinarily see things. Contemplating reality is about bringing our thinking home, to the heart. As well as trying to be more continually attentive, we greet everything that comes to our attention as an introduction to some aspect of reality. For example, non-dual experience is an essential basis for insight, but one doesn't get there by imagining non-duality. One prepares for it by taking in more carefully the straightforward duality of one's way of looking at things, by becoming aware of the lines one is always unconsciously drawing between oneself (or the various groups of family or tribe with which one identifies) and the world that lies outside that constantly shifting magic circle.

We may try to reflect upon how things decay and die, we may try to observe how we ourselves decay and die, but observing ourselves in this way still leaves the self triumphantly secure, observing. To contemplate impermanence itself is really impossible. All we can do is contemplate ourselves as we try futilely to create permanence out of houses, jobs, relationships, and all the rest of it. By patiently stripping away our repeated attempts to cover up the indecent fact of our own mortality with a blanket of abstractions, we steadily begin to corner reality even before we get a glimpse of it.

What we contemplate in this kind of meditation is how we go about experiencing and responding to things. Contemplating reality sounds very grand, but it is just a matter of becoming clearer about what we think of as ordinary reality. One may contemplate conditionality – that is, how things arise in dependence upon conditions, how nothing exists in isolation – but the point of this practice is not to get a theoretical understanding of this process, but to find it taking place in ourselves, here and now, unravelling everything upon which the mind tries to fix itself.

When we are on our own, with nothing to do, we naturally give ourselves up to daydreams and distractions. But there is something more interesting we can do. We can turn things over in our minds, question the assumptions and concepts that guide the way we live. What do we really believe in? What do we put our heart into? Where do we find our joy? In this way, we turn over the mind as a gardener works the earth, breaking up the ground to make it more fertile.

The teachings of Buddhism exist less to provide answers than to provide the tools and the light by which we may investigate ourselves at ever deeper levels. Thus meditative concentration takes our reflections further by refining our conceptualizations. To take a simple example, in the Metta Bhavana, you may start by verbalizing – 'May she be well' but the words should gradually soften until eventually you are in some sense saying the words without them crossing your consciousness at all. In the same sort of way, the breakthrough to insight comes when your thinking has become so subtle and refined that understanding shifts subtly into insight, like the shift from thinking about something to simply seeing it. It is analogous to how, when you become really concentrated on your breath, your consciousness of the breath itself seems to disappear.

The essential prerequisite for insight practice is concentration. It is said that trying to develop insight without concentration is like trying to keep a candle alight in a draughty room. Cognitive activity in dhyana is more refined than our everyday mind – more penetrating, intuitive, positive, flexible, and aware – and these qualities are intensified if they are imbued with the flavour of the experience of the higher dhyanas. But the higher dhyanas are not where insight actually takes place; insight meditation is practised most effectively at the level of the first dhyana, where we are still connected to our ordinary experience through conceptual thinking (which is not present in the higher dhyanas), or in 'access concentration', the concentrated state that precedes the arising of the first dhyana.

The Buddha's original problem was that however deeply he experienced his own nature in meditation, when he emerged from those heavenly realms of dhyana he found that the reality of his nature could not be

separated from the reality of others, that it was con-
structed in the world outside the matrix of his meditation practice. He discovered that reality could not be
found within the separate experience of the self, however refined or godlike this might be. In order to gain
insight, the fully integrated mind has to surrender that
divine self-sufficiency. (From the Buddhist point of view,
the Christian myth of God incarnating in the human
realm as the Christ may be said to symbolize this necessary process.) The Buddha designed his mindfulness
practice specifically so that the concentrated mind could
establish a critical engagement with the world that
would unpick the fabric of its delusion and suffering.

The other major prerequisite for insight is faith: to wait
without any expectation or hope – for hope, as T.S. Eliot
says, would be hope for the wrong thing – in the confidence that insight will reveal itself to us, like watching
for a rare bird to dart before us. If we have decided to
contemplate a Buddhist doctrine like the four noble
truths, for example, we stop trying to understand them,
and just deepen our receptivity to them. Reality is not to
be understood according to any categories, and as we
habitually understand things by categorization, this
leaves us unable to take any steps towards it, or even to
invite it. Instead, we can become aware of an ever-
increasing build-up of pressure as our gradually clarify-
ing perspective on reality bears down on our deep but
ever more vulnerable emotional investment in the way
we usually see things.

That scrawny cry – it was
A chorister whose C preceded the choir.
It was part of the colossal sun,
Surrounded by its choral rings,
Still far away. It was like
A new knowledge of reality.
Wallace Stevens, 'Not ideas about the thing but the thing itself'

The arising of transcendental insight is not like having an idea or even an ordinary insight. It seems to come not from inside oneself but from outside. It is not something that one's own mind comes up with. It is not a concept or even an emotion, nor is it necessarily a blinding flash, or a road-to-Damascus experience. Visionary experience may contain an element of insight, or it may not. A deep sense of faith, joy, even fear may have the perfume of transcendental insight, or it may not. This insight is perhaps most likely to emerge simply as a subtle yet powerful sense of some fundamental and inexplicable shift in one's being.

We protect ourselves, and our sense of our own centrality, by reading the world rather than living it, by clinging to the idea of the thing rather than experiencing the thing itself. Actually to see another person is a tremendous threat to our own centrality. To go out to meet the world and engage with it directly rather than through the mediation of our ideas, our prejudices, our religion, leaves us with nothing really secure. But this is the open heart of Buddhist meditation. And it is a wise and happy heart.

MEDITATION POSTURES

Meditating in Burmese posture

Kneeling astride cushions

FURTHER READING

Kamalashila, *Meditation*, Windhorse, Birmingham 1996 (a
    clear and comprehensive guide to basic Buddhist
    meditation).

Ayya Khema, *Being Nobody, Going Nowhere*, Wisdom,
    Somerville USA, 1987 (few good writers on Buddhism
    have this German Theravadin nun's depth of spiritual
    experience).

Joanna Macy, *Mutual Causality in Buddhism and General
    Systems Theory*, SUNY, New York 1991 (a brilliant
    illumination of the fundamental principle of Buddhist
    thought).

Nanamoli, *The Life of the Buddha*, Buddhist Publication
    Society, Kandy 1992 (a classic collection of translations
    from the Pali suttas).

Sangharakshita, *The Taste of Freedom*, Windhorse, Birmingham
    1997 (radical insights into the fundamentals of Buddhist
    practice).

Sangharakshita, *Who is the Buddha?* Windhorse, Glasgow 1994.

Sangharakshita, *What is the Dharma?* Windhorse, Birmingham 1998 (more from the author's own teacher).

Shunryu Suzuki, *Zen Mind, Beginners Mind*, Weatherhill, New York 1999 (profound teachings on Soto Zen meditation).

Sogyal Rimpoche, *The Tibetan Book of Living and Dying*, Rider, London 1998 (a beautiful and imaginative summation of a great teacher's understanding of the Tibetan approach to death).

The Windhorse symbolizes the energy of the enlightened mind carrying the Three Jewels – the Buddha, the Dharma, and the Sangha – to all sentient beings.

Buddhism is one of the fastest-growing spiritual traditions in the Western world. Throughout its 2,500-year history, it has always succeeded in adapting its mode of expression to suit whatever culture it has encountered.

Windhorse Publications aims to continue this tradition as Buddhism comes to the West. Today's Westerners are heirs to the entire Buddhist tradition, free to draw instruction and inspiration from all the many schools and branches. Windhorse publishes works by authors who not only understand the Buddhist tradition but are also familiar with Western culture and the Western mind. Manuscripts welcome.

For orders and catalogues contact

WINDHORSE PUBLICATIONS	WINDHORSE BOOKS	WEATHERHILL INC
11 PARK ROAD	P O BOX 574	41 MONROE TURNPIKE
BIRMINGHAM	NEWTOWN	TRUMBULL
B13 8AB	NSW 2042	CT 06611
UK	AUSTRALIA	USA

Windhorse Publications is an arm of the Friends of the Western Buddhist Order, which has more than sixty centres on five continents. Through these centres, members of the Western Buddhist Order offer regular programmes of events for the general public and for more experienced students. These include meditation classes, public talks, study on Buddhist themes and texts, and 'bodywork' classes such as t'ai chi, yoga, and massage. The FWBO also runs several retreat centres and the Karuna Trust, a fund-raising charity that supports social welfare projects in the slums and villages of India.

Many FWBO centres have residential spiritual communities and ethical businesses associated with them. Arts activities are encouraged too, as is the development of strong bonds of friendship between people who share the same ideals. In this way the FWBO is developing a unique approach to Buddhism, not simply as a set of techniques, less still as an exotic cultural interest, but as a creatively directed way of life for people living in the modern world.

If you would like more information about the FWBO visit the website at www.fwbo.org or write to

LONDON BUDDHIST CENTRE	ARYALOKA
51 ROMAN ROAD	HEARTWOOD CIRCLE
LONDON	NEWMARKET
E2 0HU	NH 03857
UK	USA

ALSO FROM WINDHORSE

BODHIPAKSA

VEGETARIANISM

Part of a series on *Living a Buddhist Life*, this book explores connections
between vegetarianism and the spiritual life.

As a trained vet, Bodhipaksa is well placed to reveal the suffering of
animals in the farming industry, and as a practising Buddhist he can identify
the ethical consequences of inflicting such suffering. Through the Buddhist
teaching of interconnectedness he lays bare the effects our eating habits can
have upon us, upon animals, and upon the environment.

He concludes that by becoming vegetarian we can affirm life in a very clear
and immediate way, and so experience a greater sense of contentment,
harmony, and happiness.

112 pages
ISBN 1 899579 15 X
£4.99/$9.95

VESSANTARA

THE MANDALA OF THE FIVE BUDDHAS

The mandala of the Five Buddhas is an important Buddhist symbol – a
multi-faceted jewel communicating the different aspects of Enlightenment.
Meeting each Buddha in turn, we start to awaken to the qualities they
embody – energy, beauty, love, confidence, and freedom.

By contemplating the mandala as a whole we can transform ourselves
through the power of the imagination, and experience the majesty of the
mind set free.

96 pages, with colour plates
ISBN 1 899579 16 8
£5.99/$11.95

PARAMANANDA

CHANGE YOUR MIND:
A PRACTICAL GUIDE TO BUDDHIST MEDITATION

Buddhism is based on the truth that, with effort, we can change the way we are. But how? Among the many methods Buddhism has to offer, meditation is the most direct. It is the art of getting to know one's own mind and learning to encourage what is best in us.

This is an approachable and thorough guide to meditation, based on traditional material but written in a light and modern style. Colourfully illustrated with anecdotes and tips from the author's experience as a meditator and teacher, it also offers refreshing inspiration to seasoned meditators.

208 pages, with photographs
ISBN 0 904766 81 0
£8.99/$17.95

KAMALASHILA

MEDITATION: THE BUDDHIST WAY OF TRANQUILLITY AND INSIGHT

A comprehensive guide to the methods and theory of Buddhist meditation, written in an informal style. It provides a complete introduction to the basic techniques, as well as detailed advice for more experienced meditators seeking to deepen their practice.

The author is a long-standing member of the Western Buddhist Order, and has been teaching meditation since 1976. In 1979 he helped to establish a semi-monastic community in North Wales, which has now grown into a public retreat centre. For more than a decade he and his colleagues developed approaches to meditation that are firmly grounded in Buddhist tradition but readily accessible to people with a modern Western background. Their experience – as meditators, as students of the traditional texts, and as teachers – is distilled in this book.

304 pages, with charts and illustrations
ISBN 1 899579 05 2
£13.99/$27.95

ABHAYA

LIVING THE SKILFUL LIFE

In this booklet Abhaya outlines a commonly used set of five 'training precepts', with a sympathetic commentary on each. Here we can learn the Buddhist approach to non-violence, to sex, to drugs and alcohol. Especially, we learn that Buddhist ethics are not about forsaking things that are forbidden, but embracing a positive and joyful way of living.

58 pages
ISBN 1 899579 17 6
£2.99/$5.95

KAMALASHILA

SITTING

As increasing numbers of stiff-limbed Westerners take up meditation, one all-important question arises: What is the best way to sit?

This booklet provides essential advice on the various sitting postures one can adopt, and explains how to sit comfortably without risk or harm.

A number of helpful loosening-up excercises, drawn from Hatha Yoga, T'ai Chi, Alexander Technique, and conventional 'PT' are introduced and illustrated.

36 pages, with illustrations
ISBN 0 904766 37 3
£2.50/$4.95

SANGHARAKSHITA

RITUAL AND DEVOTION IN BUDDHISM:
AN INTRODUCTION

For many people in the West, devotional practice is a confronting aspect of Buddhism which it is easier to ignore. Skilfully steering us through the difficulties we may encounter, Sangharakshita shows that ritual and devotion have a crucial role to play in our spiritual lives, because they speak the language of the heart. Leading us through the Sevenfold Puja, a poetic sequence of devotional moods, he gives us a feeling for the depth of spiritual practice to be contacted through recitation, making offerings, and chanting mantras.

Knowledge alone cannot take us far along the spiritual path. This book reveals the power of devotional practices to help us commit ourselves to spiritual change with all our hearts.

128 pages
ISBN 0 904766 87 X
£6.99/$13.95

TEJANANDA

THE BUDDHIST PATH TO AWAKENING

The word Buddha means 'one who is awake'. In this accessible introduction, Tejananda alerts us to the Buddha's wake-up call, illustrating how the Buddhist path can help us develop a clearer mind and a more compassionate heart.

Drawing on over twenty years' of Buddhist meditation and study, Tejananda gives us a straightforward and encouraging description of the path of the Buddha and his followers – the path that leads ultimately to our own 'awakening'.

224 pages, with diagrams
ISBN 1 899579 02 8
£8.99/$17.95

Meditating is based on a section from the following NAXOS Audio Book.

JINANANDA

THE MIDDLE WAY: THE STORY OF BUDDHISM
Read by David Timson with Anton Lesser and Heathcote Williams

Interest in Buddhism has never been greater. The story and teachings of a man who lived 2,500 years ago have a special resonance for us today, perhaps because he taught a way of life that was not based on belief in a creator god but on personal experience.

Jinananda, a Western-born Buddhist, divides the subject into the Three Jewels – the Buddha (the story of his life), the Dharma (the fundamental teachings of Buddhism) and the Sangha (the followers of the Buddha).

With extracts from some of the main sutras, Jinananda explains the key concepts that lie behind a system of thought and behaviour that, like the universe itself, is continually expanding.

This audio book is available as a triple CD set from Windhorse Publications.

ISBN 9 626341 46 7
£13.99